Namibia Culture and Art

Travel Guide, Tourism, Government, People and Tradition

Author
Edward Simpson

Carré 1957 Zogbo Littoral
Cotonou JB, 1015.

.

Table of Content

Author Note

Art and Culture on-**Namibia**, is intended for the following value; Educational purposes, Touristic information, Business engagements, Holiday intensive and Self-educational purpose. We intend to create awareness to people's interest on African Nations, the effort that we have made in making this project a reality is based on peoples interested areas on African environment, and we are satisfied with what we have done so far. The book pages may not be that long, if you had expected more pages, but that is not our intention, and it does not make the value of a book after-all, but providing you with a book that drives towards your need and provide you the information that make you go for it, and eventually serve you to satisfaction. **Namibia Art and Culture** information book will surely get you through.

Note! There is no image in this book, the reason for not including images is to attract a full concentration for better understanding of this book, images are just picture reference, the real attraction is the quality of the book base on the written content. Please go through our Table of Content to see the information headlines, doing so will help you make a choice, and eventually lead you through the part that you need most. Thank you.

Namibia Culture and Art

Culture

The culture of the indigenous population reflects the social values, norms, traditions and institutions developed over a long period of time. Each ethnic group has its on distinct identity though certain features remain common to all such as the wealth of traditional arts, crafts, music and dance. The German influence dominates the urban culture where from architecture to Lutheran churches and missions to beergartens and sausages, every aspect of daily life has strong Teutonic characteristics.

The many different tribes people who live within the territorial boundaries of Namibia have a range of crafts typical of each ethnic group. Traditional arts and crafts include basketry, woodcarving, leatherwork, beadwork, ceramics and painting. Some of the more recent developments in the crafts have been in the fields of textiles - hand weaving and embroidery - sculptures, printmaking and theatre.

The tribes living in the north of Namibia, like the Bushmen, Caprivians, Damara, Himba, Kavango and Owambo continue to create magical items from wood with a fine old tradition of woodcarving. Masks, figurines, bowls, instruments, sculptures and furniture are made in ornate or very simplistic styles using the decorative techniques of incising, etching, carving and burning. Leather from the skins of cattle and crocodile and other wild animals is crafted in to bags, pouches, footwear, belts, rugs (karosses) and traditional headgear used by the tribals.

The Bushmen living in and around the Kalahari Desert and the Himba tribesmen specialise in beadwork. They use beads made from as diverse substances as ostrich egg shells, porcupine quills, stones, seeds, nuts and wood. Necklaces, bracelets, armlets, anklets, headbands, bags, pouches and clothes are vividly decorated with a variety of handmade and commercially produced beads in traditional patterns. In fact, every motif and pattern has its own story and even the different coloured strips of palm leaves woven into baskets in special geometric designs have their own cultural identity and meaning.

The women from the Caprivi, Kavango and Owambo tribes are the best potters in all of Namibia. They make vessels for domestic use decorated with traditional geometric patterns in myriad hues. The Nama women utilise their old skills to create hand woven and hand embroidered linen, table linen, wall hangings, dresses and shawls. A newer craft that has become very popular with domestic and foreign shoppers are the rugs, carpets, wall hangings and stoles made from karakul lamb wool

Cultural Policy in Namibia

'Unity in diversity' is the slogan of the Namibian cultural policy established in 2001, which is based on international guidelines laid down in publications such as UNESCO's World Report on Culture. The core is that everybody is entitled to their own culture, as long it does not impinge on the rights of other cultures. The aim is to encourage and improve mutual understanding, respect and tolerance, thus achieving national unity. Much of this effort is aimed at the younger generation, with art and culture now forming an integral part of the school curriculum.

Cultural policy is seen as a unifying measure when it comes to discrimination and discord. For many decades in Namibia, discrimination based on race or culture was rampant. When the country became independent from apartheid South Africa in 1991, cultural policy was given an important role to play, as it was felt that art and culture lay at the heart of the creation, development and democratization of a nation.

Namibia is considered to be one of the most media-friendly countries in Africa. Its cultivation can be seen as an attempt to improve both cultural diplomacy and national unity. The constitution provides for press freedom, which is respected by the government. The media rights organisation 'Reporters Without Borders' says there is 'no major obstacle for the circulation of news'.

Namibian Culture has seen the influence of various cultures of the world, especially due to its diverse colonial history. For many years, racism and cultural discrimination were commonplace in the country. However, since gaining independence from Apartheid South Africa in

1991, a revival of national and ethnic culture has taken place.

Music, Arts and Performance

Before independence, European-influenced arts were relatively well-funded by private and state sources. Since independence, research on and the promotion of indigenous music, dance, oral literature, and other artistic forms has increased greatly with government support.

Instruments used while making music vary among tribes. Drums are one typical instrument in Namibian and African music and performances. Additionally, strings, flutes, marimbas, gourds and horn trumpets are used to make traditional music.

Traditional Namibian music and dance performances are common during community events such as weddings. There are also some traditional festivals, which include traditional rituals comprising arts, dance, music and storytelling.

The National Theatre of Namibia serves as a venue for both Namibian and foreign musicians and stage actors, in addition to assisting community-based drama groups. School and church groups create and stage less formal productions. Traditional dance troupes representing the various ethnic groups of Namibia perform at local and national festivals and holiday celebrations, and also participate in competitions.

Crafts & visual arts

Namibia boasts some of the world's oldest rock paintings and engravings, which have been attributed to ancestors of Bushmen. The scenes are naturalistic depictions of animals, people, hunting, battles and social rituals. Local geology determined the usage of colour in the paintings. Some are monochrome pictures in red, but many are multicoloured, using ground-up earth pigments mixed with animal fat to produce 'paints' of red, brown, yellow, blue, violet, grey, black and white.

Rock engravings have also been found, often in areas where there is an absence of smooth, sheltered rock surfaces to paint on. Some of the best examples of paintings and engravings are in the Brandberg, Twyfelfontein and Erongo areas.

However, there is more to Namibian creativity than just rock paintings. Traditional arts and crafts include basketry, woodcarving, leatherwork, beadwork, pottery, music-making and dancing. More contemporary arts and crafts encompass textile weaving and embroidery, sculptures, print-making and theatre.

To access the whole range of Namibian regional arts and crafts in one place, visit the Namibia Craft Centre. Housing over 25 stalls under one roof, as well as the Omba Gallery, this is perfect for buying crafts if time is short. Many towns have street markets selling curios, and numerous lodges have small outlets selling local arts and crafts, albeit sometimes at a rather inflated price.

For more details of Namibian arts and crafts, it may be worth contacting the Arts and Crafts Guild of Namibia (PO Box 20709, Windhoek; tel: 061 223831/252468/251422; fax: 061 252125), which was established in 1992 to unite the various craftspeople under one umbrella group for promotional purposes.

Basketry

Most baskets are made from strips of Makalani palm leaves coiled into a shape that is determined by its purpose: flat plate shapes for winnowing baskets, large bowl-shaped baskets for carrying things, small closed baskets with lids and bottle shapes for storing liquids. Symbolic geometric patterns are woven into a basket as it is being made, using strips of palm leaves dyed in dark browns, purples and yellows.

Recently, baskets have been made using strips of recycled plastic bags to wind around the palm-leaf strips or grasses. Baskets are typically woven by women and are part of the crafts tradition of the northern Namibian peoples – Caprivi, Himba, Herero, Kavango and Owambo.

The best examples are found in the northern arts and crafts cooperatives, like Khorixas Community Craft Centre; Opuwo Art Promotions (PO Box 6, Opuwo); Oshana Environment and Art Centre, in Oshiko near Oshakati; Caprivi Art Centre; Mashi Crafts, beside the B8 in Kongola; and Tsumeb Arts and Crafts.

Woodcarving

Woodcarving is usually practised by men in Namibia. Wooden objects are carved using adzes, axes and knives; lathe-turned work is not traditional. Carving, incising and burning techniques are used to decorate the wood. A wide range of woodcarving is produced: sculptural headrests, musical instruments such as drums and thumb pianos; masks, walking-sticks, toys, animal figurines, bows, arrows and quivers; domestic utensils including oval and round bowls and buckets as well as household furniture.

The northern Namibian peoples – Bushmen, Caprivians, Damara, Himba, Kavango and Owambo – have woodcarving traditions. Naturally the northern arts and crafts cooperatives have a good selection (see above), especially the Mbangura Cooperative which also specialises in wooden furniture. In addition the two street markets in Okahandja act as a national selling point for woodcarvings.

Leatherwork

Leatherwork is practised by all the peoples of Namibia. The skins of cattle, sheep and game are tanned and dyed using vegetable materials, animal fat and sometimes red ochre. The goods crafted include carrying skins and bags, tobacco pouches, karosses (to be used as rugs or blankets) and traditional clothing – head-dresses, girdles/aprons and sandals as well as more contemporary fashion accessories like shoes, boots, handbags, belts and jackets. The leatherworkers are usually women, though men also participate if large, heavy skins are being tanned or dyed. Swakopmund Tannery is an interesting place to visit to see how the hides are treated and also to buy crafted leatherwork.

Beadwork

Beadwork is traditionally the domain of the Bushman and Himba peoples. The Bushmen make beads from ostrich-egg shells, porcupine quills, seeds, nuts and branches; and also use commercially produced glass beads. The Himba people use iron beads and shells. In both peoples, men tend to make the beads and the women weave and string them into artefacts. These include necklaces, bracelets, armlets, anklets and headbands. The Bushmen also use beadwork to decorate their leatherwork bags, pouches and clothing – a particularly striking traditional design being the multicoloured circular 'owl's-eye'.

Bushman crafts are best bought either locally in the Tsumkwe area or the Tsumeb Arts and Crafts Centre. Alternatively, a more commercial outlet with a good selection is Bushman Art (179 Independence Avenue, Windhoek; tel: 061 228828; fax: 061 228971). Failing that, check for new outlets with the Nyae Nyae Development Foundation of Namibia at PO Box 9026, Eros, Windhoek tel: 061 236327; fax: 061 225997.

The Himba people also make a traditional iron-bead and leather head ornament (oruvanda) that all women wear and belts (epanda) that only mothers wear. Authentic Himba crafts are easiest to find in Kaokoland, where you will often be offered crafts by local villagers.

Pottery

Namibia's more renowned potters are women from the Caprivi, Kavango and Owambo peoples. Traditionally, geometric patterns of various colours decorate the vessels of different shapes and uses. Contemporary potters are experimenting with decoration by textures and a variety of sculptural motifs. The best selection of pottery is found at the Caprivi Arts Centre.

Textiles

Nama women traditionally used patchwork techniques when making dresses and shawls. Now these women utilise their sewing skills in the art of embroidery and appliqué, making table and bed linens, cushion covers and wall-hangings depicting Namibian animals and village scenes. Good places to buy these items include:

Textiles made by women involved in the Anin project near Uhlenhorst can be purchased both at Anib Lodge near Mariental, and at House Sandrose in Lüderitz. Other embroidered textiles, made by women involved with the Tuyakula project in Katutura, may be bought at Zoo Café in Windhoek.

Another textile craft that has recently developed is the hand-weaving of pure karakul wool into wall-hangings and rugs. The designs are usually geometric patterns or Namibian landscapes, though almost any design can be commissioned. Among the best places to see and buy these rugs and wall-hangings are Karakulia in Swakopmund and Dorka Teppiche in Dordabis.

Painting, sculpture and prints

The work of contemporary Namibian artists, sculptors and print-makers is on display (and often available for sale) in the many galleries in the urban areas. The country's biggest permanent collection is at the National Art Gallery of Namibia. This has over 560 works of art dating from 1864 to the present day. There are many landscapes and paintings of wild animals amongst the earlier works. Every two years the winning entries of the Standard Bank Biennale are exhibited here. Contemporary Namibian visual arts are exhibited at the following:

Performing arts

Dance

Traditional dancing in Namibia is a participatory activity at community gatherings and events like weddings. Hence, a visitor is unlikely to witness any, unless invited by a Namibian. However, some public performances of traditional dancing are to be seen at the Caprivi Arts Festival (held between September and November in Katima Mulilo at the Caprivi Arts Centre) and at Lizauli Traditional Village.

In Bushmanland, in villages surrounding Tsumkwe, traditional Bushman dances are performed for tourists – usually for a fee. This is generally a relaxed, uncontrived affair.

Afkawandahe and the African Performing Arts Group also perform traditional Namibian dances at the College for the Arts auditorium in Windhoek.

Performances of European dance, including ballet, take place at either the National Theatre of Namibia or at Franco-Namibian Cultural Centre.

Music

Most of the Namibian peoples have a music-making tradition – singing, and playing drums, bows, thumb pianos and harps. The Namas also have a tradition of religious singing in four-part harmony. Oruuano, the Namibian Artists' Union, recently held the first Oruuano of Namibia Arts Festival at Soweto Market, in Katutura (Windhoek), involving Namibian artists and musicians. It is hoped that this festival will become a regular occurrence.

Pre-Independence colonial influences have resulted in many Namibian musicians performing in the Western tradition. Concerts are regularly performed by Namibia National Symphony Orchestra, National Youth Choir, and touring foreign musicians in the main auditorium of the National Theatre of Namibia. This is also the venue for the Namibian Broadcasting Corporation's biennial Music Makers' Competition.

Many smaller-scale concerts take place at the Franco-Namibian Cultural Centre. Cantare Audire Choir is a classically trained chorus which performs regularly at Christus Kirche, Windhoek (ask at the church for concert details).

Jazz, reggae, mbaganga and pop bands perform at the 150-seater Warehouse Theatre and at the various bars, restaurants and clubs in Windhoek such as Club Thriller. Bands and rock groups with a larger following usually perform at the Independence Arena in Katutura, which has the capacity for 4,000 people, or alternatively at the Windhoek Country Club which can accommodate audiences of over 1,000 people. Out of Windhoek, the national tour circuit includes large venues in Swakopmund, Walvis Bay and Okahandja.

Theatre

There are many Namibian theatre companies including the Rossko Cultural Group, Dalma Productions and Caprivi Cultural Troupe. Several South African theatre companies also tour Namibia. Apart from the National Theatre of Namibia and the Warehouse Theatre, there are small studio-theatres at the John Muafangejo Arts Centre and the Space Theatre at the University of Namibia's Centre for Visual and Performing Arts. Both host avant-garde and experimental theatre performances.

The best of Namibian theatre (and other arts and crafts) can be seen at the National Arts and Cultural Festival, which takes place every

December in a different region each year. Between September and November there are smaller festivals held throughout the country to choose the regional entries.

People

Eleven ethnic groups make up the majority of the population, which is overall around two million people, with each tribe contributing its own traditions to the core of Namibian culture. The population is youthful, with 44 percent aged fourteen and under and only 4 percent aged older than 65. About 60 percent live in the far north, where rainfall is sufficient for grain farming. Most households are not nuclear families, but contain other kin as well. The head of the household manages domestic finances, makes important decisions, and organizes productive activities.

The tribes are divided as follows; About half of the population belong to the Ovambo tribe, which has several sub-tribes. Approximately 9% belong to the Kavangos tribe. Other ethnic groups are Herero (7%), Damara (7%), Nama (5%), Caprivian (4%), Bushmen (3%), Baster (2%) and Tswana (0.5%).

The oldest inhabitants, the San, are known to be great storytellers and love music, dance and mimicry. The Nama of the south have a tradition of prose and poetry and a natural talent for music. Eight Owambo sub-tribes reside in Namibia, the largest being the Kwanyama. One of the interesting features of the traditional Owambo social system is that lineage is traced through the mother and through maternal ancestors. The Herero are a pastoral cattle-breeding people. Herero women wear Victorian-style dresses adapted from the wives of Rhenish missionaries. The Himba women (of Herero descent) rub their bodies with a mixture of red ochre and fat, wear traditional body ornaments and garments, and have hairstyles that correspond to their age, sex and social status.

Namibia also has a fair number of Europeans, either Germans or Afrikaaners living in the country. The tribes still follow a traditional life style, practicing their old crafts and working at the age old traditional occupations of subsistence farming, animal husbandry, hunting or fishing. In modern Namibia, most of the tribes have lost their traditional lands, and hence are looking towards urban professions and trades. The Bushmen of the San tribe live in small nomadic groups of 25-30 members, spending their time eking out an existence from hunting and gathering of food from the forests, even though they are part of an intricate but widespread trade network.

English and Afrikaans are the two official languages of Namibia but German and Portuguese are widely spoken in areas where the

German and Portuguese influences were stronger. Indigenous languages spoken are Bantu origin languages like Owambo, Kavango, Herero, Caprivi and Tswana and the Khoisan languages spoken by Bushmen or San tribesmen and the Nama-Damara people.

Ethnic groups

When the colonial powers carved up Africa, the divisions between the countries bore virtually no resemblance to the traditional areas of the various ethnic groups, many of which therefore ended up split between two or more countries. As you will see, there are cultural differences between the groups in different parts of Namibia, but they are only a little more pronounced than those between the states of the USA, or the regions of the (relatively tiny) UK.

There continues to be a great deal of inter-marriage and mixing of these various peoples and cultures – perhaps more so than there has ever been, because of the efficiency of modern transport systems. Generally, there is very little friction between these communities (whose boundaries, as we have said, are indistinct) and Namibia's various peoples live peacefully together.

In Namibia, which is typical of any large African country, historians identify numerous ethnic groups. The main ones are detailed below, arranged alphabetically. Apart from Afrikaans, their languages fall into two main families: Khoisan and Bantu. The population sizes given are based on surveys done during the 1980s, and adjusted according to estimated average growth rates since then.

Caprivian

The Caprivi people live in the fertile, swampy land between the Chobe and Zambezi rivers – at the eastern end of the Caprivi Strip. Their language is of the Bantu family. Like the

Kavango and the Owambo, they farm a variety of crops, raise livestock, and fish. The agricultural potential of the area is one of the highest in Namibia. However, this potential has been largely unrealised. Before the war with Angola, and the heavy involvement of South African troops (which brought roads and infrastructure), the whole of the Kavango and Caprivi region was one of the least developed in Namibia.

Caprivians make up about 4% of Namibia's population, and most can be considered as members of one of five main groups: the Masubia and Mafwe groups, and the smaller Mayeyi, Matotela and Mbukushu. Their traditional crafts include extensive use of baskets (especially fish traps, and for carrying grain), wooden masks and stools, drums, pottery, leather goods and stone carvings.

Bushmen

There is not another social/language group on this planet which has been studied, written about, filmed and researched more than the Bushmen, or San, of the Kalahari, although they currently comprise only about 3% of Namibia's population. Despite this, or indeed because of it, popular conceptions about them, fed by their image in the media, are often strikingly out of step with the realities. Thus they warrant a separate section devoted to them here.

The aim of these next few pages is to try and explain some of the roots of the misconceptions, to look at some of the realities, and to make you think. Although I have spent a lot of time with Bushmen in the Kalahari, it is difficult to separate fact from oft-repeated, glossy fiction. If parts of this discussion seem disparate, it's a reflection of this difficulty.

Recent scientific observations on the Khoisan

Our view of the Bushmen is partly informed by some basic anthropological and linguistic research, mostly applying to the Khoisan, which is worth outlining to set the scene.

Anthropology

The first fossil records that we have of our human ancestors date back to at least about 60,000 years ago in East Africa. These are likely to have been the ancestors of everyone living today.

Archaeological finds from parts of the Kalahari show that human beings have lived here for at least 40,000 years. These are generally agreed to have been the ancestors of the modern Khoisan peoples living in Botswana today. (The various peoples of the Khoi and the Bushmen are known collectively as the Khoisan. All have relatively light golden brown skin, almond shaped eyes and high cheekbones. Their stature is generally small and slight, and they are now found across southern Africa.)

Language research

Linguists have grouped all the world's languages into around 20 linguistic families. Of these, four are very different from the rest. All these four are African families – and they include the Khoisan and the Niger-Congo (Bantu) languages.

This is amongst the evidence that has led linguists to believe that human language evolved in Africa, and further analysis has suggested that this was probably amongst the ancestors of the Khoisan.

The Khoisan languages are distinguished by their wide repertoire of clicking sounds. Don't mistake these for simple: they are very sophisticated. It was observed by Dunbar that, 'From the phonetic point of view these [the Khoisan languages] are the world's most complex languages. To speak one of them fluently is to exploit human phonetic ability to the full.'

At some point the Khoisan languages diverged from a common ancestor, and today three distinct groups exist: the northern, central and southern groups. Languages gradually evolve and change as different groups of people split up and move to new areas, isolated from their old contacts.

According to Michael Main, the northern group are San and today they live west of the Okavango and north of Ghanzi, with representatives found as far afield as Angola. The southern group are also San, who live in the area between Kang and Bokspits in Botswana. The central group is Khoe, living in central Botswana, and extending north to the eastern Okavango and Kasane, and west into Namibia, where they are known as the Nama.

Each of these three Khoisan language groups has many dialects. These have some similarities, but they are not closely related, and some are different to the point where there is no mutual understanding. Certain dialects are so restricted that only a small family group speaks them; it was reported recently that one San language died out completely with the death of the last speaker.

This huge number of dialects, and variation in languages, reflects the relative isolation of the various speakers, most of whom now live in small family groups as the Kalahari's arid environment cannot sustain large groups of people living together in one place as hunter-gatherers.

In Namibia, the three main groups are the Haixom in the northern districts of Otavi, Tsumeb and Grootfontein; the !Kung in Bushmanland; and the Mbarankwengo in west Caprivi.

Genetic discoveries

Most genetically normal men have an X- and a Y-chromosome, whilst women have two X-chromosomes. Unlike the other 22 pairs of (nonsex) chromosomes that each human has, there is no opportunity for the Y-chromosome to 'swap' or 'share' its DNA with any other chromosome. Thus all the information in a man's Y chromosome will usually be passed on, without change, to all of his sons.

However, very rarely a single 'letter' in the Y-chromosome will be altered as it's being passed on, thus causing a permanent change in the chromosome's genetic sequence. This will then be the start of a new lineage of slightly different Y-chromosomes, which will be inherited by all future male descendants.

In November 2000, Professor Ronald Davis and a team of Stanford researchers claimed to have traced back this lineage to a single individual man, and that a small group of East Africans (Sudanese and Ethiopians) and Khoisan are the closest present-day relatives of this original man. That is, their genetic make-up is closest to his.

(It's a scientific 'proof' of the biblical Adam, if you like.)

This is still a very contentious finding, with subsequent researchers suggesting at least ten original male sources ('Adams') – and so although interesting, the jury remains out on the precise details of all these findings. If you're interested in the latest on this, then you'll find a lot about this on the web – start searching with keywords: 'Khoisan Y chromosome.'

Historical views of the Bushmen

Despite much evidence and research, our views of the Bushmen seem to have changed relatively little since both the Bantu groups and the first Europeans arrived in southern Africa.

The settlers' view

Since the first Bantu farmer started migrating south through East Africa, the range of territory occupied by the foragers, whose Stone-Age technology had dominated the continent, began to condense. By the time the first white settlers appeared in the Cape, the Khoisan people were already restricted to Africa's southwestern corners and the Kalahari.

All over the world, farmers occupy clearly demarcated areas of land, whereas foragers will move more and often leave less trace of their presence. In Africa, this made it easier for farmers, first black then white, to ignore any traditional land rights that belonged to foraging people.

Faced with the loss of territory for hunting and gathering, the foragers – who, by this time were already being called 'Bushmen' – made enemies of the farmers by killing cattle. They waged a guerrilla war, shooting poison arrows at parties of men who set out to massacre them. They were feared and loathed by the settlers, who, however, captured and valued their children as servants.

Some of the Khoisan retreated north from the Cape – like the ancestors of Namibia's Nama people. Others were forced to labour on the settlers' farms, or were thrown into prison for hunting animals or birds which had been their traditional prey, but which were now designated property of the crown.

This story is told by Robert J Gordon in The Bushman Myth: The Makings of a Namibian Underclass. He shows that throughout history the hunter-gathering Bushmen have been at odds with populations of settlers who divided up and 'owned' the land in the form of farms. The European settlers proved to be their most determined enemy, embarking on a programme of legislation and massacre. Many Bushmen died in prison, with many more shot as 'vermin'.

Thus the onslaught of farmers on the hunter-gatherers accelerated between the 1800s and the mid-1900s. This helped to ensure that hunter-gathering as a lifestyle only continued to be practical in marginal areas that couldn't be economically farmed – like the Kalahari. Archaeological evidence suggests that hunter-gatherer peoples have lived for about 60,000 years at sites like the Tsodilo Hills.

Western views of the Bushmen in the 1800s

Though settlers in the Cape interacted with Khoisan people, so did Europe and the US, in a very limited way. Throughout the 1800s and early 1900s a succession of Khoisan people were effectively enslaved and brought to Europe and the US for exhibition. Sometimes this was under the guise of anthropology, but usually it didn't claim to be anything more than entertainment.

One of the first was the 'Hottentot Venus' – a woman who was probably of Khoisan extraction who was exhibited around London and Paris from 1810 to 1815, as an erotic curiosity for aristocrats.

A string of others followed. For example, the six Khoisan people exhibited at the Coney Island Pleasure Resort, beside New York, and later in London in the 1880s and billed as the 'missing link between apes and men', and the 'wild dancing Bushman' known as Franz brought to England around 1913 by Paddy Hepston.

Impressions of the Bushmen from the 1950s

In the 1950s a researcher from Harvard, John Marshall, came to the Kalahari to study the !Kung San. He described a peaceful people living in harmony with nature, amidst a land that provided all their needs. The groups had a deep spirituality and no real hierarchy: it seemed like the picture of a modern Eden (especially when viewed through post-war eyes). Marshall was a natural cameraman and made a film that follows the hunt of a giraffe by four men over a five-day period. It swiftly became a classic, both in and outside of anthropological circles.

Further research agreed, with researchers noting a great surfeit of protein in the diet of the !Kung San and low birth rates akin to modern industrial societies.

Again the Bushmen were seen as photogenic and sources of good copy and good images. The lives were portrayed in romantic, spiritual terms in the book and film The Lost World of the Kalahari by Laurens van der Post. This documentary really ignited the worldwide interest in the Bushmen and led to subsequent films such as The Gods Must be Crazy. All the images conveyed an idyllic view of the Bushmen as untainted by contact with the modern world.

The reality

The reality was much less rosy than the first researchers thought. Some of their major misconceptions have been outlined particularly clearly in chapter 13 of John Reader's Africa: A Biography of the Continent. He points out that far from an ideal diet, the nutrition of the

Bushmen was often critically limited, lacking vitamins and fatty acids associated with a lack of animal fat in their diet. Far from a stable population with a low birth rate, it seems likely that there had been a decline in the birth rate in the last few generations. The likely cause for this was periods of inadequate nourishment during the year when they lost weight from lack of food, stress and the great exertions of their lifestyle.

In fact, it seems likely that the San, whom we now see as foragers, are people who, over the last two millennia, have become relegated to an underclass by the relentless advance of the black and white farmers who did not recognise their original rights to their traditional land.

The Bushmen today and the media

Though scientific thought has moved on since the 1950s, much of the media has not. The Bushmen are still perceived to be hot news.

The outpost of Tsumkwe is the centre for many of the Bushmen communities in Namibia. It's a tiny crossroads with a school and a handful of buildings, in a remote corner of northeastern Namibia. Despite its isolation, in 2001 this desert outpost hosted no less than 22 film crews. Yes, really, that's an average of almost two each month – and I'm not counting a whole host of other print journalists and photographers.

Talk to virtually any of the directors and you'll realise that they arrive with very clear ideas about the images that they want to capture. They all think they're one of the first, they think they're original, and they want to return home with images which match their pre-conceived ideas about the Bushmen as 'the last primitive hunter-gatherers'.

As an example, you'll often see pictures in the media of Bushmen hunters in traditional dress walking across a hot, barren salt pan. When asked to do these shoots the Bushman's usual comment is, 'Why, there's no point. We'd never go looking for anything there.' But the shots look spectacular and win prizes ... so the photographers keep asking for them. From the Bushmen's perspective, they get paid for the shots, so why not pose for the camera? I'd do the same!

Thus our current image of the Bushmen is really one that we are constantly re-creating. It's the one that we expect. But it's doesn't necessarily conform to any reality. So on reflection, popular thinking hasn't moved on much from Marshall's first film in the 1950s.

Current life for the Bushmen

Looking at the current lifestyle of the Bushmen who remain in the more remote areas of the Kalahari, it's difficult not to lapse into a romantic view of ignoring present realities. There are too many cultural aspects to cover here, so instead I've just picked out a few that you may encounter.

Nomads of the Kalahari

Perhaps the first idea to dispel is that the Bushmen are nomads. They're not. Bushman family groups have clearly defined territories, called a n!ore (in the Ju/'hoansi language), within which they forage. This is usually centred on a place where there is water, and contains food resources sufficient for the basic subsistence of the group.

Groups recognise rights to the n!ore, which is passed on from father to first-born son. Any visiting people would ask permission to remain in these. Researchers have mapped these areas, even in places like the Central Kalahari.

Hunter-gatherers

Any hunter-gatherer lifestyle entails a dependence on, and extensive knowledge of, the environment and the resident fauna and flora found there. In the Kalahari, water is the greatest need and the Bushmen know which roots and tubers provide liquid to quench thirst. They create sip wells in the desert, digging a hole, filled with soft grass, then using a reed to suck water into the hole, and send it bubbling up the reed to fill an ostrich egg. Water-filled ostrich eggs are also buried at specific locations within the groups 'area'. When necessary the Bushmen will strain the liquid from the rumen of a herbivore and drink that.

Researchers have observed that any hunting is done by the men. When living a basic hunting and gathering lifestyle, with little external input, hunting provides only about 20% of their food. The remaining 80% is provided largely by the women, helped by the children, who forage and gather wild food from the bush. By age twelve a child might know about 200 plant species, and an adult more than 300.

Social system

The survival of the Bushmen in the harsh environment of the Kalahari is evidence of the supreme adaptability of humans. It reflects their detailed knowledge of their environment, which provides them not only with food, but with materials for shelter and medicine in the form of plants.

Another very important factor in their survival is the social system by which the Bushmen live. Social interaction is governed by unwritten rules that bind the people in friendship and harmony, which must be maintained. One such mechanism is the obligation to distribute the meat from a large kill. Another is the obligation to lend such few things as are individually possessed, thereby incurring a debt of obligation from the borrower.

They also practise exogamy, which means they have an obligation to marry outside the group. This creates social bonds between groups. Such ties bind the society inextricably together, as does the system of gift exchange between separate groups.

Owing to the environmental constraints a group will consist of between 80 and 120 people, living and moving together. In times of shortage the groups will be much smaller, sometimes consisting of only immediate family – parents, grandparents and children. They must be able to carry everything they possess. Their huts are light constructions of grass, and they have few possessions.

Because no one owns property, no one is richer or has more status than another. A group of Bushmen has a nominal leader, who might be a senior member of the group, an expert hunter, or the person who owns the water rights. The whole group takes decisions affecting them, often after vociferous discussions.

Hunting

The Bushmen in the Kalahari are practised hunters, using many different techniques to capture the game. Their main weapons are a very light bow, and an arrow made of reed, in three sections. The arrowhead is usually poisoned, using one of a number of poisons obtained from specific plants, snakes and beetles. (Though most Bushmen know how to hunt with bows and arrows, the actual practice is increasingly uncommon when it's not done to earn money from observing visitors.)

All the hunters may be involved in the capture of large game, which carries with it certain obligations. The whole group shares in the kill and each member is entitled to a certain portion of the meat.

There are different methods for hunting small game, which only the hunter's family would usually share. One method for catching spring hares involves long, flexible poles (sometimes four metres long) made of thin sticks, with a duiker's horn (or more usually now a metal hook) fastened to the end. These are rammed into the hare's hole, impaling the animal, which is then pulled or dug out.

Trance dancing

Entertainment for the Bushmen, when things are good, usually involves dancing. During some dances, which may often have overtones of ritual or religion, the dancers may fall into a trance and collapse.

These trances are induced by a deliberate breathing technique, with a clear physiological explanation. Dances normally take place in the evening, around a fire. Then the women, children and old people will sit around and clap, whilst some of the younger men will dance around the circle in an energetic, rhythmic dance. Often this is all that happens, and after a while the excitement dies down and everyone goes to sleep.

However, on fairly rare occasions, the dancers will go into a trance. After several hours of constant exertion, they will shorten their breathing. This creates an oxygen deficiency, which leads to the heart pumping more strongly to compensate. Blood pressure to the brain increases; the dancer loses consciousness and collapses.

Damara

Along with the Nama and the Bushmen, the Damara are presumed to be the original inhabitants of Namibia, speaking a similar 'Khoi' click language (Khoisan family). Like the Nama, the Damara were primarily hunting people, who owned few cattle or goats. Traditionally enemies of the Nama and Herero, they supported the German colonial forces at Waterberg against the Herero uprisings and were awarded for their loyalty by an 'enlarged' homeland from the German authorities: Damaraland, the area adjacent to the Skeleton Coast (now the southern part of the Kunene province). Of the 80,000 Damara today, only a quarter manage to survive in this area – the rest work on commercial farms, in mines or as labourers in the towns. Damara women share the same Victorian style of dress as the Herero and Nama women.

They make up about 7.5% of Namibia's population, sharing their language with Namas. Traditionally Damara people have been thought of as miners, smelters, copper traders, stock farmers and tobacco growers; until the end of the 19th century when they moved to Damaraland and started practising agriculture.

Their traditional crafts include leather goods, glass and metal beadwork, wooden bowls and buckets, clay pipes and bowls, and more recently 'township art' such as wire cars.

Basters

These Afrikaans-speaking people are descendants of indigenous Hottentot women and the Dutch settlers who first arrived at the Cape in the early 17th century. The original 'coloured' or 'bastard' children found themselves rejected by both the white and the black communities in the

Cape, so keeping together they relocated themselves further north away from the colonialists. Proudly calling themselves 'Basters', they set up farming communities and developed their own distinct social and cultural structures.

During the 1860s, white settlers began to push into these areas so, to avoid confrontation, the Basters crossed the Orange River in 1868 and moved northwards once again. Trying to keep out of the way of the warring Hereros and Namas, they founded Rehoboth in 1871 and set up their own system of government under a Kaptein (headman) and a Volksraad (legislative council). Their support of the German colonial troops during the tribal uprisings brought them later protection and privileges.

Demands for self-rule and independence were repressed throughout this century until the Rehoboth Gebiet was granted the status of an independent state in the 1970s. This move by the South African administration was made with the aim of reinforcing racial divisions amongst the non-whites – rather like in the South African 'independent homelands'.

Today, Namibia's Basters still have a strong sense of identity and make up just under 3% of the population. Most still live and work as stock or crop farmers in the good cattle-grazing land around Rehoboth. Their traditional crafts include products like karosses (blankets), rugs, wall-hangings and cushion covers made of cured skins.

Herero

In 1904, the Herero and the Hottentots staged a massive uprising against the German colonial troops in South West Africa. It ended in a bloody massacre of over half the total Herero population at the battle of Waterberg. The few Herero that survived fled into the Kalahari, some crossing into what is now Botswana. The recently formed Herero People's Reparation Corporation, based in Washington, is currently suing the German government and two companies for £2.6 billion, with the case expected to be heard in the US courts during 2003.

Today, the Herero constitute the third largest ethnic group in Namibia, after the Owambo and Kavango – about 8% of the present population. Their language is Bantu based. In Botswana, they are a minority group inhabiting Ngamiland, south and west of the Okavango Delta.

Traditionally pastoralists, the Herero prefer raising cattle to growing crops – prestige and influence are dependent on the number of cattle possessed. Today, the majority of Namibian Hereros use their cattle-handling skills on commercial farms.

Herero women wear very distinctive long, flowing Victorian gowns and head-dresses. Multiple layers of petticoats made from over 12m of material give a voluminous look (two women walking side by side occupy the whole pavement!). Missionaries, who were appalled by the Hereros' semi-nakedness, introduced this style of dress in the 1800s. Now the Hereros continue to wear these heavy garments and it has become their traditional dress – though they will admit just how hot it is if asked.

Traditional Herero crafts include skin and leather products, basketry, jewellery and ornaments, and dolls in traditional Victorian-style dress, which are a very popular curio for visitors.

Himba

The Himba people share a common ethnic origin with the Hereros, having split from the main Herero group on the Namibia/Botswana border and moved west to present-day Kaokoland in search of available land. The place they found, however, is mountainous, sparsely vegetated and very arid. Cattle are central to their way of life, with the size of the herd an indication of wealth and prestige – but overgrazing of the poor soils is a major problem. The Himba are a minority group in Namibia (less than 1% of the population), and live almost entirely in their traditional areas in remote Kaokoland.

Traditional Himba crafts include work in skin and leather (head-dresses, girdles and aprons), jewellery (copper-wire neck-bands and bracelets), musical instruments, wooden neck-rests, basketry and pottery.

Kavango

The Kavango people share their name with the Okavango River, which forms the northern border of Namibia with Angola. Not surprisingly, they have based their traditional agricultural and fishing existence on the fertile land and good water supply afforded by this environment.

Many of the Kavango, who used to live on the northern side of the Okavango River in Angola, came south of the river into Namibia during the 1970s, 80s and early 90s. They fled from the civil war between South African-backed UNITA rebels and the Soviet/Cuban-backed MPLA regime. As a consequence, the Kavango population in Namibia more than doubled in size during the 1970s, and now forms the second largest ethnic group in the country, making up almost 10% of the population.

Closely related to the Owambos, the Kavango people are traditionally fishermen, and crop and stock farmers. Their craftwork includes woodcarving (bowls, spoons, mortars, masks, boxes and furniture), basketry, pottery, jewellery (grass bracelets and copper-bead necklaces), mats, spears, daggers, pipes, musical instruments and head-dresses.

Nama/Hottentot

The Nama people are perhaps the closest in origin to the Bushmen, traditionally sharing a similar type of 'click' or Khoisan language, the same light-coloured yellow skin, and a hunter-gatherer way of life. One of the first peoples in Namibia, their tribal areas were traditionally communal property, as indeed was any item unless it was actually made by an individual. Basic differences in the perception of ownership of land and hunting grounds led in the past to frequent conflicts with the Herero people. The 50,000 or so Nama today live mostly in the area that was Namaland, north of Keetmanshoop in the south of Namibia, mainly working on commercial farms. Nama women share the same Victorian traditional dress as the Herero and Damara women.

The Nama people make up about 5% of Namibia's population, and are traditionally stock farmers. Their crafts include leatherwork (aprons and collecting bags), karosses (mantle of animal skins) and mats, musical instruments (eg: reed flutes), jewellery, clay pots and tortoise-shell powder containers.

Other Namibians

Coloured Namibians

The term 'Coloured' is generally used in southern Africa to describe people of mixed (black-white) origin. These Coloured people maintain a strong sense of identity and separateness from either blacks or whites – though they generally speak either Afrikaans or English (or frequently both) rather than an ethnic 'African' language. They are very different in culture from any of Namibia's ethnic groups, white or black.

Most Coloureds in Namibia live in the urban areas – Windhoek, Keetmanshoop and Lüderitz. Those in Walvis Bay are mainly fishermen, and some in the south are stock farmers. Their traditional crafts centre mainly on musical instruments, like drums and guitars.

White Namibians

The first whites to settle in Namibia were the Germans who set up trading businesses around the port of Lüderitz in 1884. Within a few years, Namibia formally became a German colony, and German settlers began to arrive in ever-increasing numbers. Meanwhile, white farmers of Dutch origin (the Boers, who first settled on the African continent at the Cape in 1652), were moving northwards in search of land free from British interference, following the cession of the Dutch Cape Colony to the British government.

Following the transfer of German Namibia to South African control after World War I, Boers (Afrikaners) moved into Namibia, and soon significantly outnumbered the German settlers. The Namibian whites collectively refer to themselves as 'Southwesters' after Namibia's colonial name of South West Africa.

Namibians of European descent live mainly in urban, central and southern parts of the country – though they also own and run most of the commercial farming operations. Virtually all of the tourism industry is managed by white Namibians. They came as missionaries, traders and hunters, though are now found throughout the economy. Perhaps a legacy of colonialism, they are normally amongst the more affluent members of society.

The crafts currently produced by the whites include leatherwork (shoes, handbags, belts), German Christmas and Easter decorations, needlework (including embroidery, patchwork and clothing), printed T-shirts, costume jewellery, greeting cards and various classical European art-forms.

Expatriates

Distinct from white Namibians, there is a significant 'expat' community in Namibia. These foreigners usually come to Namibia for two or three years, to work on short-term contracts, often for either multinational companies or aid agencies. Most are highly skilled individuals who come to share their knowledge with Namibian colleagues – often teaching skills that are in short supply in Namibia

Owambo

The Owambo people (sometimes called Ovambo) are by far the largest group in Namibia and make up just over half the population. Their language, Oshivambo (sometimes known as Ambo or Vambo in Namibia), is Bantu based. The great majority live in their traditional areas – Owamboland – away from the main transport arteries in the remote far north of the country, straddled on the border with Angola. The area receives one of the highest rainfalls in the country, and supports a range of traditional crops as well as allowing good grazing for the extensive cattle herds.

Before independence, the existence of half a million indigenous Namibians on the border with (socialist) Angola seriously perturbed the

South African administration. By investing money into the region, the administration hoped to establish a protective buffer against Angola to protect the areas in the interior. The policy backfired – Owamboland became the heartland of SWAPO during the struggle for independence. The consequent harassment by the South African Defence Force, and a rapid population increase (exacerbated by a large influx of refugees from Angola), have left the area over-pressurised and undeveloped. The SWAPO government has long pledged to redress this imbalance.

Most of the Owambo belong to one of eight tribes: the Kwanyama, Ndongo, Kwambi, Ngandjera, Mbalantu, Kwaluudhi, Nkolokadhi and Eunda. Most still live in Owamboland, and have traditionally been traders and businessmen.

Traditional Owambo craftwork includes basketry, pottery, jewellery, wooden combs, wood and iron spears, arrows and richly decorated daggers, musical instruments, fertility dolls, and ivory buttons (ekipa) – worn by women and conveying their status and indicating their husband's/family's wealth.

Language

Namibia's variety of languages reflects the diversity of its peoples – black and white. Amongst the indigenous languages there are two basic language groups which bear no relation to each other, Bantu (eg: Owambo, Herero) and Khoisan (eg: Bushmen, Nama). The only language that comes close to being a lingua franca is Afrikaans.

Most black townspeople speak both Afrikaans and English in addition to their 'mother' language. In the more rural areas, Afrikaans tends to be more widely used than English (which may not be spoken at all) – despite the widespread enthusiasm felt for the latter. In the farming areas of the central region, German is also commonly found, as many of the commercial farmers are of German origin.

Following independence, one of the new government's first actions was to make English Namibia's only official language (removing Afrikaans and German). This step sought to unite Namibia's peoples and languages under one common tongue ('the language of the liberation struggle'), leaving behind the colonial overtones of Afrikaans and German. This choice is also helping with international relations and education, as English-language materials are the most easily available.

There isn't the space here to include a detailed guide to Namibia's many languages, although, if you are staying in a community for longer than a few days, then you should try to learn a few local greetings from your hosts. Whilst travelling, you are likely to come across unfamiliar words that are in common use in southern African English, many of Afrikaans origin.

Most Namibians speak Bantu languages like Oshiwambo and Otjiherero as their first language. Others speak Khoisan languages (Nama/Damara and various Bushman languages). Afrikaans is the most widely spoken language, which became popular as a common language during occupation. German is spoken by most of the white population. However, English is the official language, and is mainly spoken by young people and urban dwellers.

Food and Living

Rice is the staple food of the Namibians supplemented by fish, game and forest produce or vegetables. Most of the tribesmen continue to hunt and a variety of animal meat and fish is served on the tables in Namibian households and restaurants.

Happily for an African country, standards of hygiene are very high and cleanliness is a virtue found in restaurants without hunting far and wide. Most of the restaurants are modern, clean and serve mostly foreign cuisines only a few will serve African, especially Namibian food. German, French, Austrian, Swiss, Italian, Greek,

Portuguese, Taiwanese and Chinese dishes are common to menus in most restaurants.

Seafood, game meats like venison, wild boar, ostrich, zebra, crocodile steaks and beef and mutton are readily available, cooked in European/Asian styles rather than in keeping with African culinary traditions. Some of the distinctly Namibian items served in a few places are dishes using the game meat in season with Kalahari truffles or amajowa mushrooms.

From the Germans and Afrikaaners comes the European method of smoking meat and Rauchfleisch, smoked game served with melons is the Namibian version of Parma ham and melon. Restaurants in the coastal areas like Swakopmund feature grilled or poached steenbras and kabeljou caught in the off shore waters as well as shark meat, lobster and oysters.

Namibian beers and South African wines are regular favorites with most patrons of bars and pubs in Namibia. Spirits, liqueurs and wines are imported from South Africa and Germany and Scotch whisky and other alcohol from different countries ensuring a plentitude of good drinks

Important occasions are marked by the slaughter of cattle or goats, and the consumption of meat, home-brewed beer, purchased beverages, and other foods. In some cultures, leftover meat is sent home with the guests.

The typical Namibian diet and home is usually varied by geographical location and profession. Agriculturalists' staple diet are millet and sorghum. Beans and greens are eaten with millet in the north, but otherwise few vegetables are grown or consumed. Pastoral farmers mainly consume dairy products, but for some, hunting and gathering is still a means of getting food.

Additionally, some insects are part of traditional cooking. Insects have been widely used across Southern Africa and form an important aspect of many people's diets. A large mopane worm that feeds on the mopane tree leaves is considered a delicacy by rural and urban populations in Southern Africa and beyond.

The mopane worm forms the basis for traditional food, especially in the northern part of Namibia. The mopane worm is said to be one of Southern Africa's six economically important insects, with great potential for quick development.6 However, trade is threatened by over-harvesting, and mopane worms are now rare or extinct in some areas where they were once common. In order to safeguard the next crop, perhaps it is vital to leave enough of the worms to complete the life cycle by forming moths and laying eggs, thus ensuring the future of the industry. Caterpillars are also seen as an important source of protein. Most of the caterpillars are dried so that they can be stored for use throughout the year. Dried caterpillars may be eaten dry as a snack or re-hydrated and cooked in a little water before they are fried in oil with onion, tomato and chili to be eaten as a sauce relish. They are usually served with pap (maize or mahangu meal porridge).

Namibia Tourism

As the rays of the rising sun transform the sand dunes to a glorious deep red, flocks of flamingoes take to the sky in a blur of pink and the myriad calls of wild animals break the quiet of an African morning, Namibia wakes up to a new day. Drills buzz their way into the belly of the earth in search of rich booty, traffic hurtles along the nation's highways and planes take off as people go about the daily business of life in the fast lane but time stands still in the countryside where nature reigns supreme in all her majesty.

Despite its transition into the modern world of cell phones, satellites and skyscrapers, Namibia has retained its ancient character and traditions and its multi-ethnic tribal culture. A young nation that has made all the right moves to preserve and protect its environment, Namibia has vast open spaces with spectacular natural wonders like the unusual coastal Namib Desert, the deep bowl of Etosha, abundant wildlife and the stunning grandeur of the Fish River Canyon, idyllic Bavarian style villages in an African ambience and the mysteriously eerie Skeleton Coast where hot African and cold Arctic temperatures marry to lure ships to an untimely end.

Namibia's contrasting landscapes hide awesome phenomena such as the world's largest underground lake aptly named Dragon's Breath; the Hoba Meteorite, the largest chunk of extraterrestrial rock to be found on earth; the tallest dunes of red sand at Sossusvlei where wind patterns seem to be frozen for eternity and the hospitable Namib Desert that strangely sustains elephants, lions, giraffes and rhinos, as well as the oldest living fossil tree on earth, the Welwitschia Mirablis. Such unusual enchantments coupled with abundant sunshine, political and economic stability and a well-developed tourism infrastructure attracts tourists from across the globe.

Namibia, Gem of Africa, has something to offer to every soul- World's biggest deserts, national parks, tropical forests and savannahs and many more natural wonders and amazing places. There is simply no limit!

Getting around in Namibia

By Air: Most of the important urban centres in Namibia have airports or registered landing strips. Domestic connections don't cost a great deal and are definitely more popular than the train connections. Eros airport in Windhoek city serves as the hub for domestic connections and some flights from Cape Town and the many charter flights. Domestic destinations are available between Walvis Bay, Keetmanshoop, LÃ¼deritz, Oranjemund, Tsumeb, Ondangwa, Katima Mulilo and Mokuti. Internal connections are not very frequent, so need to be booked well in advance. Eros has no public transport but fortunately, the airport is very close to the city (4km) and taxis can be summoned by phone.

By Road: The low density of population in Namibia is one reason why an extensive internal bus service is not feasible, but certain well-populated areas do have regular bus and luxury coaches connecting them to other centres. Minibuses ply on the main routes, charge reasonable fares but wait till they have a full complement of passengers. Trans-Namib operates bus services from main towns on rail routes to centres without a passenger train service such as LÃ¼deritz and Grootfontein. One company operates a fleet of luxury vehicles on long-distance routes and their buses are air conditioned, comfortable and fast with refreshments, music, videos and toilet facilities. Taxi services are available on call (not on the streets) in the major cities and the city bus services are pretty efficient.

The many car rental companies that offer visitors sedans, cars, motorbikes and 4WDs on rent make up the lacuna in the public transport system. But rental charges are steep and petrol is an expensive commodity. Traffic regulations are strictly enforced a traffic drives on the left hand side of the road; a speed limit of 120 km/h on open roads should be adhered to and safety belts are mandatory. Overseas visitors but not residents of neighbouring countries must have a valid international drivers license before they can drive in Namibia.

By Train: More than 2400 km of railway lines of the Trans-Namib Railways connect the major towns in the country Windhoek is the main transport hub with passenger trains connecting it to Tsumeb, Swakopmund, Walvis Bay, Gobabis and Keetmanshoop with stops at the town enroute. One of the highlights of the tourist trade in Namibia is the ˜Desert Express a 5-star luxury overnight train service between Windhoek and Swakopmund. The South African Rovos Rail also travels a tourist circuit of over 2600km round trip from Johannesburg to Swakopmund. The Starline rail service, run by Trans-Namib is exclusively for passengers with economy and business classes but no dining cars. The trains are fairly comfortable though slow because of the many stops along the way.

Driving in Namibia

Driving yourself around Namibia is, for most visitors, by far the best way to see the country. It is much easier than driving around Europe or the USA: the roads are excellent, the traffic is light, and the signposts are numerous, clear and unambiguous.

Further, if you choose to visit private camps or concession areas, you can then use the skills of the resident guides to show you the wildlife. You're not restricted to the car, to be in it every day. Driving yourself gives you freedom to explore and to go where you like, when you like.

It's generally easiest to hire a vehicle for your whole time in Namibia, collecting it at the airport when you arrive, and returning it there when you depart. This also removes any worries that you may have about bringing too much luggage (whatever you bring is simply thrown in the boot on arrival).

However, if your budget is very tight then you may think about just taking a vehicle for a few days, perhaps from Windhoek to Swakopmund via the Sesriem area, or to drive around Etosha. However long you keep the vehicle, the type you choose and the company you hire from can make an enormous difference to your trip.

Eating Out in Namibia

The restaurants, cafes and bars in Namibia are well equipped to satisfy all kinds of taste buds from the adventurous to the parochial. Germany's long-term dominance is reflected in the restaurants and beer bars that serve continental and German cuisines. A medley of native African cuisines including the Namibian is also available at the innumerable grills, cafes and in house restaurants in clubs and hotels.

International fast food chains, familiar names serving familiar food dot the urban landscape catering to the locals and to those visitors who want to stick with the tried and tested.

South African wines, beers and lagers and other alcoholic drinks are easily available at licensed bars, pubs and restaurants carrying the YYY' and YY signs.

Namibia doesn't really have a scene for an active nightlife even though nightclubs open and shut down with uncanny regularity in Windhoek.

Best Time to Visit Namibia

Though often regarded as a year-round destination, the best time to visit most areas of Namibia is between April to October.

Marking the end of the wet summer season, the months of April and May are the harbingers of the cool and dry winter months in Namibia, and are a good time to visit as the landscape remains lush from the prior rains and the air begins to become more pleasant and calm. An advantage of travelling during these transitory months is the relatively lesser crowd which one encounters, as the heavy number of tourists are yet to arrive.

The peak season though is between end May to October. Being the winter months, temperatures start to fall, dropping to freezing point on some nights in parts of the desert areas. The lack of rainfall during these months allows for easier movement around the region as well as better game viewing across Namibia's many national parks, as the dry weather forces animals to the few water-holes and the relatively shrivelled up vegetation makes it easier to spot the same.

Most areas of Namibia are ideal to visit between these months including Windhoek, Southern Namibia, the inlands of The Namib and Skeleton Coast as well as the northern zone of Ethosha. Due to the increased demand during these months, be sure to book well in advance, as early as April for July/ August travel.

Most of Namibia is best avoided during its wet season, between December to March. Though the region receives relatively lesser rainfall than its surrounding countries, these months tend to be off-peak season, as the thunderstorms restrict movement around the region and most national parks too may shut down, owing to the poor game viewing during this period.

If visiting Namibia during the summer months, between November to March it may be better to travel to the coastal areas, namely the Skeleton Coast and The Namib. While the climate in Namibia during these months is generally warm and humid, with expected rainfall especially during the months of January and February, these coastal areas tend to be relatively cooler and may offer a good respite from the heat of the inland areas.

A piece of travel advice: If visiting around the time of Namibia's school holidays, advance bookings are advised as domestic travellers fill up the hotels. Local Holidays are between (April 25"May 25, August 15"September 5 and December 5"January 15).

Sightseeing in Namibia

There are varieties of options for sightseeing in Namibia. Start your sightseeing tour from the capital city of Windhoek! Windhoek was the former stronghold of the main opposition to German colonisation. A modern city at an altitude of 11650m, its distinct colonial architecture shows the overwhelming German influence. The centre of the city has a major shopping centre the administrative building and the main tourist centre with two fine museums, the State Museum and the Owela Museum housed in one in the oldest building in Namibia, the Alte Feste.

Swakopmund is the favourite playground of Namibians and the country's premier holiday resort. Its quaint German colonial buildings, palm trees and verdant greenery enhance the charm of this basically desert town. The town has numerous good hotels, pensions, restaurants and coffee shops selling traditional continental pastries and cakes while the coastline and desert offer great opportunities for some R&R.

Swakopmund presents the holidaymaker with uncluttered beaches and warm waters good for swimming, surfing and fishing. Anglers can try their skill from shore or in the deep seas against local species that offer a real challenge, species like the kabeljou, kingklip, monk and sole.

Walvis Bay is a busy port on the Swakopmund, bordered by sand dunes with a large fish processing industry and salt works. It's a tourist destination, particularly favoured for its bird sanctuary where 20,000 flamingo and other fresh water and coastal birds nest in the lagoon. Enroute is Bird Island, a favourite roost for coastal birds and a prolific source of guano for fertilizer.

Luderitz is a town reminiscent of Bavarian hamlet with its quaintly pastel coloured houses, laid back ambience and slow lifestyle. Its clean, isolated beaches along the Luderitz peninsula are home to a variety of marine life. The Luderitz Museum is worth the visit along with other building like the Goerke Haus, the old train and the Concert & Ball Hall fine examples of German colonial architecture.

The Namib Desert

The Namib Desert is said to be the oldest in the world and is an awesome place with its vast brooding desolate expanse, high dunes and bleak red sandscape. The Namib lies along the coastline and has extremely unusual features like the Skeleton Coast in the north, the Diamond Coast in the south and the spectacular Sossusvlei in the heart of the Namib.

As the cold currents of the Arctic marry up with the warm temperatures of the African mainland, it creates pea-soup fogs so dense that early Portuguese sailors referred to the Skeleton Coast as the ˜coast of hell lying in wait to wreck unsuspecting ships. The Diamond Coast hides a rich underbelly of diamonds, such large deposits that it makes Namibia the world's biggest producer of rough diamonds. This highly mysterious coast is now the site of the Namib-Naukluft National Park.

Sossusvlei is one of Namibia's most spectacular natural wonders. Situated 400 km northwest of the canyon in the deepest heart of the Namib Desert is this enormous clay-pan, surrounded by high sand dunes. The sands of the Namib are a harsh red and the reddish dunes rising as high as 300m are an incredible and absolutely unforgettable sight. This part of the Namib was opened to travellers as recently as 1997, and naturalists, nature lovers and photographers travel here to catch the awesome play of colours. The rare times when the pan fills with water is even more inspiring for camera enthusiasts.

The Caprivi and the Okavango are the two main wetlands areas around the River Okavango and its delta offshoots, the Linyanti and the Chobe Rivers. It is an area rich in wildlife with riverbanks and lagoons full of a variety of birds and animals. The region has many designated conservation areas like the Khaudum, Mahango, Mamili and Mudumu National Parks, home to elephant, buffalo, hippo, lechwe, puku and many more. Just short rides from the Caprivi area but across the border are the impressive Victoria Falls.

National Parks

Etosha National Park is popular as one of Africa's very best and most beautiful national parks. ˜Etosha loosely translates as the Place of Mirages, Land of Dry Water or the ˜Great White Place because of its vast pan of silvery-white sand where dust devils whirl around and mirages shimmer in the dry desert heat.

The most distinctive feature of Etosha is the enormous shallow depression - Etosha Pan, which probably is the huge bowl of an erstwhile inland lake, long dry but once fed by the River Kunene. The edges of the saltpans are mopane savannah stretching to the south, west and north, with mostly dry woodlands in the east.

The "Haunted Forest" in the east is a dense stand of gnarled moringa trees that grow only in Namibia.

Etosha has a huge population of African wild life best seen during the late summer months when they are forced to visit the few waterholes not dry. Fortunately for the animals and the tourists, there are many such waterholes in the park.

More than 340 species of birds including many rarely seen members of the raptor family, elephant, giraffe, eland, blue wildebeest, kudu, gemsbok, springbok, impala, steenbok, and zebra are protected within the limits of Etosha National Park.

Daan Viljoen Game Park is in a small park just an hour's driving time from Windhoek. The park lies in the midst of rolling hills in the Khomas Hochland, a highland area with savannah type vegetation and a willow-shaded dam, tailor-made for picnics.

The 40 sq km contains a limited amount of wildlife; notable amongst them are steenbok, springbok, gemsbok, kudu, red hartebeest, blue wildebeest, eland, baboon, mountain zebra and more than 200 species of birds. There are no large predators in the park, making it ideal for walking round and exploring on foot.

The Fish River Canyon National Park is actually a long jagged ravine 161 km long, 27 km wide and up to 549 meters deep. The canyon is numbered as one of the best hiking and trekking areas in the world as its almost lunar arid landscape is one of the last surviving tracts of true wilderness. Ai-Ais Hot Springs are hot springs beneath the peaks of the southern end of Fish River Canyon from where hot water is piped to a series of baths.

The Skeleton Coast National Park: The Kunene River and the Ugab River form the natural boundaries of the park in the north and south respectively. The Skeleton Coast derives its name from the bleached bones of shipwrecked sailors that dot its length and breadth. When the icy cold Benguela Ocean current from the Arctic meets with the warm temperatures of the African continent, it gives rise to a dense coastal fog that caused ships to flounder on the rocky outcrops, thus developing a very unsavoury reputation as shipwrecks along its coast increased in numbers.

The attraction of this dangerous area lies in the colours, changing moods and pristine virginal landscape that metamorphoses from expanses of wind swept dunes to rugged canyons with walls of multi-hued and multi-layered volcanic rock to extensive mountain ranges.

Shopping in Namibia

Namibia is one of the world's largest producers of diamonds and gemstones and diamond, tourmaline, aquamarine, amethyst, rose quartz, agate, tiger's eye and topaz jewellery are sold by licensed dealers at jewellery stores in Windhoek and Walvis Bay. Other attractions are desert rose, crystals and the rare iridescent tiger's eye. Gemstones cost a lot even though Namibia is a producer but the quality is assured. It is strongly recommended that no diamonds or gems be bought from unauthorized vendors " it is illegal and a cognizable offence under Namibian law.

Ethnic crafts like original paintings, coats, wall hangings, carpets and rugs made from karakul lambswool, kudu-leather shoes and karosses or rugs made of animal skin and fur, basket ware, wood carvings, dolls in traditional Herero-style dresses are sold at the many crafts centres across the country. Notable amongst them are places like the Caprivi Arts Centre and the Mbanguru Woodcarvers Cooperative. In the predominantly tribal belt in the Kavango and Caprivi region, some excellent bargains can be picked up at the roadside stalls selling local crafts

Where to Stay in Namibia

Namibia has a plethora of places to stay in ranging from sleek luxury hotels in the urban centres to pensiones, guesthouses, rustic farms and wildlife lodges and rest camps. Budget travellers can stay in hostels or try out the very reasonably priced but comfortable B&B places run by families in their own homes on an informal basis.

Accommodation in Namibia is officially graded according to the services offered. One star rating means the hotel offers adequate, standard facilities while two and three stars are progressively better. Four star grading is for the top end hotels that offer the maximum facilities and have the best rooms and service. Guest farms are given from one to three stars, ranging from good through very good to excellent. The "T" sign signals accommodation mainly for tourists. "YYY" is given to places like pubs and bars that are fully licensed while the twin "YY" stands for a restaurant with a permit to serve alcohol only with meals.

Bush camping & walking

Camping

Many manuals have been written on survival in the bush, usually by military veterans. If you are stranded with a convenient multi-purpose knife, then these useful tomes will describe how you can build a shelter from branches, catch passing animals for food, and signal to the inevitable rescue planes which are combing the globe looking for you – whilst avoiding the attentions of hostile forces.

In Namibia, camping is usually less about surviving than about being comfortable. You will usually have much more than the knife: at least a bulging backpack, if not a loaded vehicle. Thus the challenge is not to camp and survive, it is to camp and be as comfortable as possible. Only practice will teach you this, but a few hints might be useful for the less experienced African campers.

Walking in the bush

Walking in the African bush is a totally different sensation from driving through it. You may start off a little unready – perhaps even sleepy for an early morning walk – but swiftly your mind will awake. There are no noises except the wildlife, and you. So every noise that isn't caused by you must be an animal; or a bird; or an insect. Every smell and every rustle has a story to tell, if you can understand it.

With time, patience, and a good guide you can learn to smell the presence of elephants, and hear when impala are alarmed by a predator. You can use ox-peckers to lead you to buffalo, or vultures to help you locate a kill. Tracks will record the passage of animals in the sand, telling what passed by, how long ago, and in which direction.

Eventually your gaze becomes alert to the slightest movement, your ears aware of every sound. This is safari at its best. A live, sharp, spine-tingling experience that's hard to beat and very addictive. Be careful: watching animals from a vehicle will never be the same for you again.

The Central Passageway

Despite Windhoek's dominance of the country's central region, remember that it occupies only a small area. The city doesn't sprawl for miles. Drive just 10km from the centre and you will be on an open highway, whichever direction you choose. The recent completion of the trans-Kalahari Highway means that you can drive directly from Walvis Bay right across this region to South Africa's northern heartland, without leaving tarmac. In time, this may have a major impact on the area.

This chapter concentrates on this central swathe of Namibia, working outwards from Windhoek – to the edges of the Namib-Naukluft National Park in the west, and to the border with Botswana in the east.

The sub-sections of this chapter are:

From Windhoek to the Coast

Travelling from Windhoek to the coast, there's a choice of three obvious roads: the main tarred B2, the C28 and the more southerly C26. Along these roads there are several towns of interest to visit such as Okahandja, Karibib and Usakos.

East from Windhoek

Gobabis is busy town, standing at the centre of an important cattle farming area on the western edges of the Kalahari, forms Namibia's gateway into Botswana via the Buitepos border post, about 120km east. It's an ideal place to use the banks, fill up with fuel or get supplies before heading east towards Ghanzi, where most goods aren't so easily available. From here cross the border into Botswana - the Buitepos border opens 07.00–17.00 and is suitable for 2WD vehicles. There's little on the other side apart from a border post until you reach the small Kalahari cattle-farming town of Ghanzi.

South from Windhoek

Rehoboth is just north of the Tropic of Capricorn and 87km south of Windhoek on the tarred B1, Rehoboth is the centre of the country's Baster community, which is quite different from any of Namibia's other ethnic groups, and jealously guards its remaining autonomy. However, there are few reasons to stop here, other than the museum, and most people just pass on through.

Kavango & Caprivi Strip

The north of Namibia is generally very lush, watered by a generous annual rainfall. East of Owamboland – which means northeast of

Grootfontein – lie the regions of Kavango and Caprivi.

These support a large population, and a surprising amount of wildlife. The wildlife has visibly increased in the national parks here in the last few years, helped enormously by various successful community-based game-guard and conservation/development programmes.

The main B8 road across the strip, or Golden Highway as it is sometimes called, is now completely tarred. It is destined to become an increasingly important artery for trade with Zimbabwe and Zambia, and hence a busier road. It has come a long way since the dusty gravel road that I first crossed in 1989, when many viewed it as terra incognita.

Unlike much of the rest of Namibia, the Kavango and Caprivi regions feel like most Westerners' image of Africa. You'll see lots of circular huts, small kraals, animals and people carrying water on their heads. These areas are probably what you imagined Africa to be like before you first arrived. By the roadside you'll find stalls selling vegetables, fruit, or woodcarvings, and in the parks you'll find buffalo hiding in the thick vegetation. This area is much more like Botswana, Zimbabwe, or Zambia than it is like the rest of Namibia. This is only what you'd expect if you look at a map of the subcontinent, or read the history of the area: it really is very different from the rest of Namibia.

Note Unrest in the last few years has meant that, at times, vehicles travelling across the Caprivi strip have been proceeding in convoy. Since the situation tends to change, check the Foreign Office website, www.fco.gov.uk/travel/namibia, for up-to-date advice. Note that it is the area to the north of the Golden Highway where disturbances tend to occur.

Luderitz

Though the European colonisation of Namibia started in this southwestern corner, this remains perhaps Namibia's least known area for visitors. At the end of a long road, Lüderitz is now being rediscovered, with its wonderful turn-of-the-century architecture, desolate beaches, and position as the springboard for trips into the forbidden area, the Sperrgebiet.

But there is more than Lüderitz in this area. Early historical sites from the 1900s are dotted throughout the region – and though places to stay are often far apart, most of the hotels and guest farms are excellent value. Best of all are the amazing landscapes. Rugged mountains and flowing desert sands make the empty roads spectacular – with the D707, the southern sections of the C13, and even the main B4 across the Koichab Pan ranking amongst the country's more dramatic drives

Namib-Naukluft N. P.

People have different reactions when they encounter a desert for the first time. A few find it threatening, too arid and empty, so they rush from city to city, through the desert, to avoid spending any time there at all. Some try hard to like it for those same reasons, but ultimately find little which holds their attention. Finally there are those who stop and give the place their time, delighting in the stillness, strange beauty, and sheer uniqueness of the environment. The desert's changing patterns and subtly adapted life forms fascinate them, drawing them back time after time.

Covering almost 50,000km2, the Namib-Naukluft National Park is one of the largest national parks in Africa, protecting one of the oldest deserts on earth, South America's Atacama Desert being the other contender for this title. The Namib's scenery is stunning, and its wildlife fascinating; you just need to make the time to stop and observe it.

The sections in this chapter run roughly south to north. Note that the NamibRand, Sesriem, the Naukluft and Solitaire are very close together.

North-central

While Etosha is the main attraction in the north of Namibia, the region south of it has much of interest. Large farms dominate these hilly, well-watered highlands, and many have forsaken cattle in favour of game, to become guest farms that welcome tourists. Okonjima Guest Farm has been one of the first of these, and is a major draw for visitors. Many of the others are less famous, but they still offer visitors insights into a farmer's view of the land, and opportunities to relax. On the eastern side of this area, the Waterberg Plateau is superb, though more for its hiking trails and scenery, and feeling of wilderness, than for its game viewing.

Owamboland

This verdant strip of land between Etosha and the Kunene and Okavango rivers is largely blank on Namibia's normal tourist map. However, it is highly populated and home to the Owambo people, who formed the backbone of SWAPO's support during the struggle for independence. The region was something of a battleground before 1990, and now the map's blank spaces hide a high concentration of rural people practising subsistence farming of maize, sorghum and millet.

Before independence this area was known as Ovamboland, and recently it has been split into four regions: Omusati, Oshana, Ohangwena and Oshikoto. Here, for simplicity, I will refer to the whole area as Owamboland. During the summer Owamboland appears quite unlike the rest of Namibia. It receives over 500mm of rain and supports a thick cover of vegetation and extensive arable farming.

The Owambo people are Namibia's most numerous ethnic group, and since independence and free elections their party, SWAPO, has dominated the government. Much effort is now going into the provision of services here. There are two main arteries through Owamboland: the B1/C46, and the smaller C45. The small towns that line these roads, like trading posts along a Wild West railroad, are growing rapidly.

Alongside the main B1 there is a canal – a vital water supply during the heat of the dry season. Driving by, you pass women carrying water back to their houses, while others wash and children splash around to cool off. Occasionally there are groups meeting in the shade of the trees on the banks, and men fishing in the murky water. Some have just a string tied to the end of a long stick, but others use tall conical traps, perhaps a metre high, made of sticks. The successful will spend their afternoon by the roadside, selling fresh fish from the shade of small stalls.

Always you see people hitching between the rural towns, and the small, tightly packed combi vans, which stop for them: the local bus service. If you are driving and have space, then do offer lifts to people; they will appreciate it. It's one of the best opportunities you will get to talk to the locals about their home area.

Owamboland has three major towns – Oshakati, Ondangwa and Ruacana – and many smaller ones. With the exception of Ruacana, which was built solely to service the big hydro-electric power station there, the others vary surprisingly little and have a very similar atmosphere.

There is usually a petrol station, a take-away or two, a few basic food shops, a couple of bottle stalls (alias bars) and maybe a beer hall. The fuel is cheaper at the larger 24-hour stations, in the bigger towns, and you can stock up on cold drinks there also. The take-aways and bars trade under some marvellous names: Freedom Square Snack Bar, Music Lovers Bar and the Come

Together Bar, to name but a few. These can be lively, friendly places to share a beer, but a word of warning: they are not recommended for lone women visitors.

Away from the towns, the land seems to go on forever. There are no mountains or hills or even kopjes – only feathery clumps of palm trees and the odd baobab tree break the even horizon. After a year of good rains, the wide flat fields are full of water, like Far Eastern rice paddies, complete with cattle wading like water buffalo.

Travelling eastwards and slightly south, towards Tsumeb, notice how, as the land becomes drier, the population density decreases, and maize becomes the more dominant crop. Where the land is not cultivated, acacia scrub starts gradually to replace the greener mopane bushes by the roadside. Keep your eyes open for raptors – especially the distinctive bateleur eagles that are common here.

Towards the edge of Owamboland, at Oshivelo (about 150km from Ondangwa and 91km from Tsumeb), you must stop to pass through a veterinary cordon fence. This is just a kilometre north of the bed of the Omuramba Owambo, which feeds into the Etosha pan.

Skeleton Coast

By the end of the 17th century, the long stretch of coast north of Swakopmund had attracted the attention of the Dutch East India Company. They sent several exploratory missions, but after finding only barren shores and impenetrable fogs, their journeys ceased. Later, in the 19th century, British and American whalers operated out of Lüderitz, but they gave this northern coast a wide berth – it was gaining a formidable reputation.

Today, driving north from Swakopmund, it's easy to see how this coast earned its names of the Coast of Skulls or the Skeleton Coast.

Treacherous fogs and strong currents forced many ships on to the uncharted sandbanks that shift underwater like the desert's sands. Even if the sailors survived the shipwreck, their problems had only just begun. The coast here is but a barren line between an icy, pounding ocean and the stark desert interior. The present road (C34) runs more or less parallel to the ocean, and often feels like a drive along an enormous beach – with the sea on one side, and the sand continuing forever on the other.

For the first 250km or so, from Swakopmund to about Torra Bay, there are almost no dunes. This is desert of gravel and rock. Then, around Torra Bay, the northern dune-sea of the Namib starts, with an increasingly wide belt of coastal dunes stretching north to the Kunene River. But nowhere are these as tall, or continuous, as the Namib's great southern dune-sea, south of the Kuiseb River.

At first sight it all seems very barren, but watch the amazing wildlife documentaries made by the famous film-makers of the Skeleton Coast, Des and Jen Bartlett, to realise that some of the most remarkable wildlife on earth has evolved here. Better still, drive yourself up the coast road, through this fascinating stretch of the world's oldest desert. You won't see a fraction of the action that they have filmed, but with careful observation you will spot plenty to captivate you.

Flora and fauna

Sand-rivers

A shipwrecked sailor's only hope on this coast would have been to find one of the desert's linear oases – sand-rivers that wind through the desert to reach the coast. The Omaruru, the Ugab, the Huab, the Koichab, the Uniab and the Hoanib are the main ones. They are few and far between. Each starts in the highlands, far inland, and, although normally dry, they flood briefly in years of good rains. For most of the time their waters filter westwards to the sea through their sandy beds. Shrubs and trees thrive, supporting whole ecosystems: green ribbons which snake across seemingly lifeless plains.

Even in the driest times, if an impervious layer of rock forces the water to surface, then the river will flow overland for a few hundred metres, only to vanish into the sand again as swiftly as it appeared. Such watering places are rare, but of vital importance to the inhabitants of the area. They have allowed isolated groups of Himba people to stay in these parts, whilst also sustaining the famous desert populations of elephant and black rhino.

In many of these river valleys there are thriving populations of gemsbok, kudu, springbok, steenbok, jackals, genets and small wild cats. The shy and secretive brown hyena is common, though seldom seen. Giraffe and zebra are scarce residents, and even lion or cheetah will sometimes appear, using the sand-rivers as alleys for hunting forays. Lion used to penetrate the desert right to the coast to prey on seals. Although it is many years since the last such coastal lion was seen, rising game populations in the interior are encouraging a greater population of lion in the region, so perhaps we'll see individuals on the beaches again before too long.

Beside the sea

Outside the river valleys, the scenery changes dramatically, with an outstanding variety of colours and forms. The gravel plains – in all hues of brown and red – are bases for occasional coloured mountains, and belts of shifting barchan sand-dunes.

Yet despite their barren appearance, even the flattest of the gravel plains here are full of life. Immediately next to the sea, high levels of humidity sustain highly specialised vegetation, succulents like lithops, and the famous lichens – which are, in fact, not plants at all but a symbiotic partnership of algae and fungi, the fungi providing the physical structure, while the algae photosynthesise to produce the food. They use the moisture in humid air, without needing either rain or even fog. That said, frequent coastal fogs and relatively undisturbed plains account for their conspicuous success here.

In some places lichens carpet the gravel desert. Take a close look at one of these gardens of lichen, and you'll find many different species, varying in colour from bright reds and oranges, through vivid greens to darker browns, greys and black. Most cling to the rocks or the crust of the gypsum soil, but a few species stand up like the skeletons of small leafless bushes, and one species, Xanthomaculina convolute, is even windblown, a minute version of the tumbleweed famous in old Western films.

All come alive, looking their best, early on damp, foggy mornings. Sections appear like green fields of wispy vegetation. But if you pass on a hot, dry afternoon, they will seem less interesting. Then stop and leave your car. Walk to the edge of a field with a bottle of water, pour a little on to a small patch of lichens, and stay to watch. Within just a few minutes you'll see them brighten and unfurl.

Less obvious is their age: lichens grow exceedingly slowly. Once disturbed, they take decades and even centuries to regenerate. On some lichen fields you will see vehicle tracks. These are sometimes 40 or 50 years old – and still the lichens briefly crushed by one set of wheels have not re-grown. This is one of the main reasons why you should never drive off the roads on the Skeleton Coast.

Further inland

East of the coastal strip, between about 30 and 60km inland, the nights are very cold, and many mornings are cool and foggy. However, after about midday the temperatures rocket and the humidity disappears. This is the harshest of the

Namib's climatic zones, but even here an ecosystem has evolved, relying on occasional early-morning fogs for moisture.

This is home to various scorpions, lizards, and tenebrionid beetles, living from wind-blown detritus and vegetation including dune-creating dollar bushes, Zygophyllum stapffii, and perhaps the Namib's most fascinating plant, the remarkable Welwitschia mirabilis.

West Coast Rec. Area

The coast is divided into three areas. North of Swakopmund up to the Ugab River, covering about 200km of coast, is the National West Coast Tourist Recreational Area. No permits are needed to drive through here and there are a few small towns and several campsites for fishing parties.

Getting there

It is even more vital here than in the rest of Namibia: you need a vehicle to see this part of the Skeleton Coast. Hitchhiking is not restricted, but with bitterly cold mornings and desiccating afternoons it won't be pleasant – heat exhaustion would be a real danger. A few tour companies in Swakopmund run excursions to Cape Cross, about 120km or 11/2 hours' drive from Swakopmund which stop at one of the lichen fields, and some of the more obvious sites of interest on the way.

By far the best method is to drive yourself, equipped with plenty of water and a picnic lunch, and stop where and when you wish to explore. Set off north as early as possible, catching the southern sections of the road in the fog, and pre-book to stay at Terrace Bay for the night. The drive alone will take about five hours, though most people stop to explore and have refreshments, and so make a whole day of it.

The main C34 is tarred up until the C35 turn-off, just north of Henties Bay. After that it becomes what is known locally as a salt road, made of salt, gypsum and gravel compacted hard over the years. It has no loose surface, and so is almost as solid and safe as tar. You can drive faster on this than you would on normal gravel, though it sometimes twists around and gets bumpy – so there's no leeway for a lack of concentration.

Skeleton Coast Park

Costs: N$20 per adult, N$1 per child, plus N$20 per car.

From the Ugab to the Kunene, the Skeleton Coast Park and Wilderness Areas protect about one-third of the country's coastline. The southern half of this, the Skeleton Coast Park, is easily accessible to anyone with a car and some forward planning. It's a fascinating area and, surprisingly, is often omitted from scheduled tours and safaris. This is a shame, though it does mean that from July to September – when some of the rest of the country is busy with overseas visitors – this is still a blissfully quiet area.

Getting there

Because the climate here is harsh, and the area quite remote, the Ministry of Environment and Tourism have fairly strict regulations about entry permits – which must be followed.

If you are just passing through, then you can buy your entry permit at either gate: the Ugab River gate on the C34, or the Springbokwasser gate on the D3245. You must reach your gate of entry before 15.00 to be allowed into the park – otherwise you will simply be turned away.

If you plan to stay at either Torra or Terrace Bay, then you must have a booking confirmation slip, issued by the main NWR office in Windhoek. You cannot just turn up at the gate, or one of the camps, to see if they have any space. You must pre-book these camps in Windhoek. In that case, if you arrive from Swakopmund along the C34, you must pass the Ugab River no later than 15.00. Similarly, if coming from Damaraland, on the D3245, you must pass the Springbokwasser gate by 17.00.

The Wilderness Area

To understand the current situation in the Wilderness Area, you need to know the recent history of the park, as well as some politics.

History

The Skeleton Coast Park was initially part of the Etosha National Park, proclaimed in 1906. Then in 1967, South Africa's Odendal Commission cut it down to 25% of its original size, making in the process several 'homelands' for the existing communities. Included amongst these were parts of what is now known as Damaraland and Kaokoland, and also the Skeleton Coast.

During the late '50s and '60s permission was granted to private companies, including one called Sarusas Mining Corporation, for mining and fishing rights on the Skeleton Coast. During the late 1960s, they assembled a project team to build a brand new harbour at Cape Frio. They did all the research and got backing from investors, but at the last moment the South African government pulled the plug on the project. After all, a new Namibian port would reduce the stranglehold that Walvis Bay had on the country – and that had historically belonged to South Africa even before it took over the administration of German South West Africa (Namibia).

The Sarusas Mining Corporation were not happy and took the case to court. Instrumental in this was the young lawyer on their team, Louw Schoemann. As part of the out-of-court settlement, the South African government agreed to allow the area to be re-proclaimed as a national park – and hence the Skeleton Coast was proclaimed as a park in 1971.

However, during the course of all this research, Louw had fallen in love with the amazing scenery and solitude of the area. He had already started to bring friends up to the area for short exploratory safaris. As word spread of these trips, he started taking paying passengers there as well.

In order to preserve part of the area in totally pristine condition, the northern part was designated as a 'Wilderness Area' – to be conserved and remain largely untouched. Strictly controlled rights to bring tourists into one part of this area were given to just one operator. Rules were laid down to minimise the operator's impact, including a complete ban on any permanent structures, a maximum number of visitors per year, and the stipulation that all rubbish must be removed (no easy task) and that visitors must be flown in.

Louw won the tender for this concession, giving him the sole right to operate in one section of the wilderness area. So he started to put his new company, Skeleton Coast Fly-in Safaris, on a more commercial footing. The logistics of such a remote operation were difficult and it remained a small and very exclusive operation. Its camps took a maximum of twelve visitors, and much of the travel was by light aircraft. The whole operation was 'minimum impact' by any standard. Louw was one of the first operators to support the pioneering community game-guard schemes in Namibia and he maintained a very ecologically sensitive approach long before it was fashionable.

I travelled to the coast with Louw in 1990. It was spellbinding; one of the most fascinating four days that I've spent anywhere. Partly this was the area's magic, but much was down to the enthusiasm of Louw, and the sheer professionalism of his operation.

Gradually, Skeleton Coast Fly-in Safaris had become a textbook example of an environmentally friendly operation, as well as one of the best safari operations in Africa. Louw's wife, Amy, added to this with the stunning photographs in her book, The Skeleton Coast. The latest edition of this (see Further Reading) is still the definitive work on the area. His sons, André and Bertus, joined as pilot/guides, making it a family operation. In many ways, Louw's operation put the area, and even the country, on the map as a top-class destination for visitors. Fly-in safaris to the Skeleton Coast had become one of Africa's ultimate trips – and largely due to Louw's passion for the area.

Politics in the 1990s

In 1992, the new government put the concession for the Skeleton Coast Wilderness Area up for tender, to maximise its revenue from the area. No local operator in Namibia bid against Louw; it was clear that he was operating an excellent, efficient safari operation in a very difficult area – and such was the operation's reputation, no local company would even try to bid against them.

However, a competing bid was entered by a German company, Olympia Reisen, headed by the powerful Kurt Steinhausen, who have extensive political connections in Namibia and Germany. They offered significantly more money, and won the concession. (They subsequently built the enigmatic Oropoko Lodge, near Okahandja)

Local operators were uniformly aghast. Suddenly a foreign firm had usurped Namibia's flagship safari operation. Negative rumours of Olympia Reisen's other operations did nothing to allay people's fears.

Inevitably given his legal background, Louw started legal proceedings to challenge the bid. However, the stress of the situation took its toll and tragically he died of a heart attack before the case was heard. The challenge succeeded, but Olympia Reisen appealed to the High Court, who referred the matter to the cabinet. The cabinet set aside the ruling, and awarded the concession to Olympia Reisen for an unprecedented ten years. Olympia Reisen's political connections had won through.

The rules of the game had clearly changed. The monthly 'rent' for the concession that Skeleton Coast Safaris used to pay has been abolished. In its place, Olympia Reisen pays the government N$1,000 for every visitor taken into the concession. However, with no 'rent' and no minimum number of visitors, the government's income from the area dropped drastically. In the first four years of Olympia Reisen's operation they carried fewer than 400 people into the concession – less than half the number of visitors taken in annually by Skeleton Coast Safaris.

Olympia Reisen is widely viewed with suspicion in Namibia, and conspiracy theories abounded about what they were doing up on such a remote stretch of coast where nobody could watch their operations. Their negative attitude to journalists, including myself, did nothing to help counter the rumours.

The current situation

By the mid-1990s it was becoming clear that Olympia Reisen were never going to make a commercial success of safaris to the area, and whilst they were there, nobody else could see the area. Finally in 1999, Wilderness Safaris – a major player in southern Africa with a good reputation for sensitive development and responsible operations – became involved. They made a deal with Olympia Reisen to take control of tourism in the area.

They ripped down the poor structures that Olympia Reisen had erected, removed from the area numerous truckloads of accumulated rubbish, and set about a series of ecological impact assessments prior to opening a totally new Skeleton Coast Camp in April 2000. They also took control of all the ecological monitoring in the area, effectively putting an end to the many rumours about what had been happening in the wilderness area – and ultimately providing a base for a number of wildlife researchers who now have projects in the area. The tender for this area is again due to be up for bidding at the end of 2003. Given the excellent track record of the current operation, and the difficulty of working in this area at all, Wilderness Safaris is widely expected to retain the concession.

Meanwhile, after losing the rights to use the Skeleton Coast Wilderness area to Olympia Reisen in 1992, the Schoeman family continued to operate their own fly-in safaris. They did this using remote areas of the Skeleton Coast just south of the wilderness area, and parts of the western Kaokoveld and Damaraland just east of the park's boundary. Although they were slightly different areas of the coast and its hinterland, their style and guiding skills remained as strong as ever – and their trips remained superb. On several occasions I've spoken with travellers that

I've sent on these trips who have been full of praise and described them as 'life-changing experiences'

Surviving the Namib

Where To Find Life?

The Namib Desert receives its stingy allotment of water in two ways. Its eastern edges, near the escarpment, get rare showers of rain. There you will find inselbergs which can store the water for a time and support permanent communities of perennial plants and resident animals. At the coast, the desert's western edge, the annual rainfall is even lower (less than 5mm at Walvis Bay), and there most organisms rely on the fogs which regularly roll in from the sea. However, in the middle of the desert where neither the rain nor fog reach, there is very little life indeed.

By Escaping

Many of the Namib's species can only survive at all if they either escape or retreat from the extremes. An 'escape' is an extended period of absence from the desert community, such as a suspension of the life cycle, aestivation (the desert equivalent of hibernation), or by actually migrating out of the desert.

Many of the Namib's plants stop their life cycle for particularly harsh periods, leaving behind dormant seeds able to withstand temperatures of up to 100°C and remain viable for years. Growth is eventually triggered by a threshold amount of rainfall, leading to the phenomenon of the 'desert bloom', where a carpet of flowers covers the ground. These plants, called ephemerals, must then complete their life cycles in a matter of days before the water disappears. A blooming desert obviously requires its pollinators, so various insect species also conduct ephemeral life cycles, switching them on and off as rainfall dictates.

On the great plains of the Namib, a different community waits for rain in any slight depression. When it arrives, and the depression fills, an explosion of activity occurs and pond life comes to the desert. Algae, shrimps and tadpoles fill the ponds for their short lives, employing rapid development techniques to swiftly mature to adulthood.

Large-scale migrations are not common in the Namib, but springbok do trek between arid regions, following any rain, and the Namib's largest mammal, the gemsbok, also moves in a predictable pattern. They move into the Namib's dune-sea after rainfall, looking for the ephemeral grasses. When these vanish, they travel to the dry Kuiseb River bed to compete with the resident baboons for acacia pods and water. Here they excavate waterholes, which they maintain from year to year.

By Retreating

A 'retreat' is a short term escape, typically a matter of hours. This has a serious disadvantage: it results in what ecologists call a 'time crunch', where time for foraging and social activity is greatly reduced. It follows that retreating animals must be very efficient at foraging.

Most species retreat to some extent. The Namib's beetles, reptiles, birds and mammals disappear into burrows and nests during the hottest periods of the day. One of the most visible is the social weaver bird, which builds enormous communal nests which insulate the birds during cold nights, and provide a handy retreat during the heat of the day.

In order to extend the time spent on the surface, and minimise this time crunch, one Namib resident, the sand-diving lizard, has developed the remarkable behaviour of 'dancing' on the surface. By lifting its legs at intervals, (never all at once!), it manages to reduce its body temperature and stay out for a few extra minutes of activity.

Although some form of escape or retreat is practical for most animal species, plants do not have the same luxury. They cannot move quickly and therefore have to become tolerant.

Specialised Plants

Most of the Namib's plants have very deep root systems, to acquire what little ground water is available, and adaptations to reduce water loss. Their leaves are usually small and often covered in hairs or a waxy coating. These designs all reduce water loss by evaporation. Smaller leaves mean less surface area, hairs trap still air adjacent to the leaf and waxy coatings don't allow moisture to pass through. The swollen, waxy leaves of succulents are filled with water, and hence must be protected from thirsty grazers. They usually employ toxins, or spines, but in the Namib there are also the extraordinary geophytes, plants which camouflage themselves as stones. Add to the problem of desiccation that of overheating. Most desert plants are orientated to minimise heating, by having their narrowest edge facing the sun. Some geophytes go one better by growing almost entirely underground.

Animal Adaptations

Water, the ultimate limitation of the desert, is of key importance to the Namib's animals. Without exception, all of the animal species here tolerate extreme levels of desiccation, and some employ interesting techniques. The male namaqua sandgrouse travels miles to find water each day. When successful, he paddles in it, allowing his breast feathers to absorb water like a sponge. Laden with this cargo he travels back to the nest to feed the thirsty young and his partner. Springboks and gemsbok have kidneys that are so efficient at absorbing water that a pellet form of urine is produced.

The African ground squirrel faces away from the sun at all times, and uses its tail as a parasol while it forages. Perhaps most peculiar to the Namib are the dune beetles, which inhabit the crests of the desert's taller sand-dunes. They are early risers when there is fog about, and sit motionless for hours in order to allow it to condense on their bodies. Periodically they perform a spectacular dance to move the precious water along their bodies and into their mouths.

The seals

In mid- to late-October the large males, or bulls, arrive, their massive body weight of around 360kg far exceeding that of the 75kg females. They stake their territorial claims and try to defend them from other males. Shortly afterwards, in late November or early December, each of the pregnant females gives birth to a single pup. These will remain in and around the colony, and continue suckling for the next ten or eleven months.

Shortly after giving birth, the females mate with the males who control their harems, and the cycle continues, with the pups born about a year later. When the females have all given birth, and mated, most of the males will leave to break their fast and replenish the enormous amounts of body-fat burned whilst defending their territories. In the last few months of the year, the scene can be quite disturbing, with many pups squashed by the weighty adults, or killed by the area's resident populations of jackal and brown hyena.

Southern Kalahari & Fish River Canyon

If you have journeyed north from South Africa's vast parched plateau, the Karoo, or come out of the Kalahari from the east, then the arid landscapes and widely separated towns of southern Namibia will be no surprise. Like the towns, the region's main attractions are far apart: the Fish River Canyon, Brukkaros, the

Quivertree Forest, and scattered lodges of the Kalahari.

Perhaps because of their separation, they recei

ve fewer visitors than the attractions further north, so if you want to go hiking, or to sleep out in a volcano, or just to get off the common routes – then this southern side of the country is the perfect area to.

The major sections this chapter are:

Mariental

Despite being the administrative centre of the large Hardap Region, which stretches from the Atlantic coast to Botswana, Mariental still avoids being a centre of attention by having remarkably few attractions. It is central and pleasant, with a sprinkling of efficient businesses serving the prosperous surrounding farmlands.

Hardap Dam Recreational Resort

About 250km from Windhoek, and less than 25km from Mariental, lies the Hardap Dam, creating Namibia's largest man-made lake. This dams the upper reaches of the Fish River to provide water for Mariental and various irrigation projects. It is surrounded by a small reserve, complete with restcamp.

East of Mariental and the b1: the Kalahari

The Kalahari Desert often surprises people when they first see it. It is very different from the Namib. First of all, remember that the Kalahari is not a true desert: it receives more rain than a true desert should. The Kalahari is a fossil desert. The Kalahari's dunes are very different. They are often equally beautiful, but usually greener and less stark – and with this vegetation comes the ability to support more flora and fauna than a true desert.

The road from Mariental to Keetmanshoop

Between Mariental and Keetmanshoop is a 221km stretch of tar road that most visitors see at speed. However, a few places are worth knowing about as you hurry past:

Keetmanshoop

Keetmanshoop lies about 480km south of Windhoek at an altitude of 1,000m. The tar roads from Lüderitz, South Africa and Windhoek meet here, making it the hub of southern Namibia's road network, as well as the administrative centre of this region.

The Deep South

South and east of Keetmanshoop, Namibia's central highlands start to flatten out towards the South Africa's Karoo, and the great sand-sheet of the Kalahari to the east. Many of the roads here are spectacular: vast and empty with enormous vistas.

Fish River Canyon

At 161km long, up to 27km wide, and almost 550m at its deepest, the Fish River Canyon is probably second in size only to Arizona's Grand Canyon – and is certainly one of Africa's least-visited wonders.

Windhoek

Namibia's capital spreads out in a wide valley between bush-covered hills and appears, at first sight, to be quite small. Driving from the international airport, you pass quickly through the suburbs and, reaching the crest of a hill, find yourself suddenly descending into the city centre.

As you stroll through this centre, the pavement cafés and picturesque old German architecture conspire to give an airy, European feel, whilst street-vendors remind you that this is Africa. Look upwards! The office blocks are tall, but not sky scraping. Around you the pace is busy, but seldom as frantic as Western capitals seem to be.

Leading off Independence Avenue, the city's main street, is the open-air Post Street Mall, centre of a modern shopping complex. Wandering down it, between its bright, pastel-coloured roofs, you'll find shops selling everything from fast food to fashion. In front of these, street-vendors crouch beside blankets spread with jewellery, crafts and curios for sale. Nearby, the city's more affluent residents step from their cars in shaded parking bays to shop in air-conditioned department stores.

Like many capitals, Windhoek is full of contrasts, especially between the richer and poorer areas, but it lacks any major attractions. For casual visitors the city is pleasant; many stop for a day or two, as they arrive or leave, though few stay much longer. It is worth noting that the city all but closes down on Saturday afternoons and all day Sunday, so be aware of this if you plan to be in town over a weekend. Note, too, that during the holiday season from Christmas to around

January 10, large numbers of locals leave for the coast, leaving many shops, restaurants and tourist attractions closed. That said, this is the centre of Namibia's administration, and the hub of the country's roads, railways and communications. If you need an embassy, good communications, or an efficient bank, then Windhoek is the right place for you. And to prepare for a trip into the bush, Windhoek is by far the best place in Namibia to get organised and buy supplies

Health and safety

There is always great danger in writing about health and safety for the uninitiated visitor. It is all too easy to become paranoid about exotic diseases that you may catch, and all too easy to start distrusting everybody you meet as a potential thief – falling into an unfounded us-and-them attitude toward the people of the country you are visiting.

As a comparison, imagine an equivalent section in a guidebook to a Western country – there would be a list of possible diseases and advice on the risk of theft and mugging. Many Western cities are very dangerous, but with time we learn how to assess the risks, accepting almost subconsciously what we can and cannot do.

It is important to strike the right balance: to avoid being excessively cautious or too relaxed about your health and your safety. With experience, you will find the balance that best fits you and the country you are visiting.

Climate

Even though a large part of the landmass of Namibia lies in the tropics, the country actually experiences an archetypal desert type climate with hot, dry days and cooler nights. Most of the country is classified as arid, semi arid or desert and only 8% of the entire country receives plenty of rain. Rainfall is minimal and erratic in most parts like the coastal Namib Desert, which receives an annual precipitation of 51mm, the inland areas receive 152mm of rainfall but the sub-humid region receives over 500mm of annual rainfall. Between end October and early

April, the country gets rain on clouds borne by the northeast winds.

The extremely unpredictable rainfall ensures high temperatures throughout the year. Summer and winter temperatures see a great deal of variation with average mean temperatures in the range of 35Â°- 42Â°C across the country except for slightly cooler areas like the highlands and the coastal plain. In the Okavango and the Kalahari basin temperatures soar up to 40.8Â° to 47.8Â°C respectively while Walvis Bay, Windhoek and the Central highlands are a wee bit cooler at 35Â° -36Â°C.

The Kalahari basin, Okavango, Caprivi and the Orange River trough are the hottest parts of Namibia. October is the warmest month in northern Namibia, December in the highlands and January along the coast and in the south. July is the coldest month for the large part of the country while August is the coolest month along the coast. In the winters, night temperatures can fall as low as -5°C.

Economy

Introduction

Namibia possesses an economy based mainly on the primary sector and boosted by the export of minerals, producing large quantities of uranium, tin, tungsten, lead and zinc. Namibia is also one of the world's leading exporters of gem-quality Diamonds, which represents a large proportion of its GDP.

In 2010, according to the International Monetary Fund, the GPD of Namibia was US$ 11,450,000,000.00, with the GDP per capita amounting to US$5,454.00, thus making Namibia a low-middle income economy. The mining sector employs only 3% of Namibia's population, therefore forcing approximately half of the Namibian population to make a living from subsistence agriculture.

The impact of the 2008 financial crisis on the Namibian economy with regards has been to diminish the GDP growth prospects for the upcoming years. In 2007, the Namibian government had predicted the growth of the GDP - between 2008 and 2012 - to be an average of 5.2% per annum, which, due to the crisis, was not achieved. Instead, in 2008 the Namibian economy grew only 4.8% instead of the expected 5.2%.

As part of the Common Monetary Area – also including Lesotho, South Africa and Botswana – the Namibian economy depends heavily on South Africa. Both the Rand and the Namibian Dollar are legal tender in Namibia, however, the latter is not accepted in South Africa. Moreover, the actions of the Bank of Namibia are always based upon the regulations of the South African

Central Bank. Due to its close relations to South Africa, Namibia enjoys certain privileges, the most obvious of these being the Rand and the Namibian Dollar having a 1:1 parity, which has prevented, in the past few years, the depreciation of the Namibian currency.

Before independence, the South African administration controlled the economy along traditional colonial lines. The country produced goods it did not consume but imported everything it needed, including food. Namibia still exports maize, meat and fish, and imports rice and wheat. However, although about 60% of the workforce is employed in agriculture, the country's commercial agriculture is limited by water, while large sections of wetter northern regions are already farmed intensively by subsistence farmers.

Namibia inherited a well-developed infrastructure and considerable remaining mineral wealth. Mining is the mainstay of the economy, accounting for about 25% of the country's GDP. There are important reserves of uranium, lead, zinc, tin, silver, copper and tungsten, as well as very rich deposits of alluvial diamonds. There are plans, too, to tap into the Kudu gas field, in the South Atlantic Ocean off Namibia's southern coast.

Tourism also plays an important role in the formal economy. Tourism to Namibia remains small-scale, but has been growing steadily by about 15% per year since 1993. Statistics for arrivals from overseas in 1997 indicate about 28,000 visitors from the UK, 14,000 from the USA, and 80,000 from Germany. Namibia has tremendous potential for sustained growth in tourism, provided the increases are steady and well managed.

Namibia's main attractions for visitors are stunning scenery, pristine wilderness areas and first-class wildlife. As long as the country remains safe and its wilderness areas are maintained, then the country's potential for quality tourism is unrivalled in Africa. Already tourism is a powerful earner of foreign exchange and a vital support for numerous local community development schemes.

Economically, Namibia remains dependent on South Africa; its other main trading partners are Germany, Switzerland and the UK.

Since the country is still establishing its own industries, it meets most if its needs for manufactured goods by importing them from South Africa. Realistically, the economy is likely to stay closely involved with that of South Africa, especially while Namibia continues to peg its currency to the value of the South African rand.

The revenue and foreign exchange from mining provides the financial muscle for the government's agenda. The government is developing structural changes to make the economy more equitable, and to diversify its components. Better living conditions for the majority of Namibians are being realised by increasing the productivity of the subsistence areas, particularly in the populated north. However, there remains an enormous gap between the rich and the poor, which must be closed if the country is to have a secure and prosperous future.

Trade

According to the Ministry of Trade and Investment, in order to promote economic growth, Namibia should focus on export-oriented strategies through the increase of trade diversification of products and trading partners.

The African Economic Outlook 2010 by OECD shows that over the period 2008-2009, due to the global economic crisis, exports dropped from 35,6 % to 31,8 % of GDP, while imports increased from 23,7 % to 39,7 % of GDP, leading to a change in the trade balance from a surplus in 2008 to a deficit in 2009.

Namibia is part of the SACU, "Southern African Customs Union", and of the SADC, "Southern African Development Community", economic unions of southern African states, also including South Africa, which is the largest trading partner of Namibia (recipient of 31,8 % of Namibian exports and origin of 67,8 % of Namibian imports). The Free Trade Agreement between the SACU and the EFTA states fosters trade partnerships with European countries, with the UK accounting for 15% of Namibian exports.

Foreign Investment

Several factors contribute to making Namibia one of the most attractive African countries for investment and businesses. First of all, ever since it became an independent and democratic state in 1990, Namibia has enjoyed political stability and good governance. In 1992, the Foreign Investments Act came into force, establishing the basis for an investment-friendly regulatory framework and establishing the "Namibia Investment Centre", the country's official investment promotion and facilitation office, which provides diverse and tailor-made services to investors. Namibia developed a reputation as one of the lowest credit risk countries in Africa, especially due to the competitive tax-based incentive regime policies.

On top of the favorable foreign investment regulation, Namibia is also part of a number of bilateral, regional and multilateral markets and trade arrangements (e.g. SADC and SACU).

In the latest UNCTAD World Investment Report (2010), Namibia is reported as the 34th country by inward FDI performance in 2009: FDI received amounts to 516 millions of dollars. Inward FDI stocks represent 42.4% of GDP, higher than the African and Developing economies averages (34.6% and 29.1% respectively).

Namibia "Vision 2030"

Following western practices, Namibia's government decided to boost its development and reconstruction of the economy by developing more advanced sectors. The project, "Vision 2030", was released in 2004 with views to provide guidelines for improvements, taking into consideration: inequalities and social welfare, peace and political stability, human resources, institution building, macro-economic issues, population, health and development, natural resources and environment, knowledge, information and technology, as well as factors of the external environment.

The overall goal of this strategic document is to move the country's development towards the standards of an industrialised nation by the year 2030. The plan aims to unlock the huge potential of this outstanding African country. The project sees Namibia as a prosperous, industrialized, peaceful and stable state developed by its human potential.

In "Vision 2030", Namibia seeks to be a globally competitive, efficient, sustainable, knowledge-based and industrialized economy. Namibia would rather be a provider of development assistance than an aid-recipient country. To achieve these goals, the government needs to implement new technologies, as well as to link science to industry. In order to do that, there are plans to establish a Science and Technology Innovation Fund.

Moreover, Namibia wants to establish business standards of competence, ethical behaviour and trust, reduce bureaucracy and maintain a transparent government. For instance, one of the government's main aims is to increase GDP until 2030 by 6 % per year, and to reduce unemployment to a 2% rate. Furthermore, the project endeavors to lessen poverty by ensuring decent employment and diminishing inequalities between the rural and urban zones with respect to racial equality, gender, age, ethnicity or political affiliation.

To achieve the aforementioned goals, Namibia aims at increasing urbanization from 31% in 2001 to 75% in 2030. The other big aspiration is to improve international policies in order to cooperate with other countries effectively. And when infrastructure is taken into consideration,

Namibia has the desire to expand its existing rail and road networks as to ensure smooth and equal development of the regions, as well as its relations with the neighboring countries.

Additionally, another target is to provide a decent living environment for all citizens, so that they can fully realise their human potential. Despite the fact that Namibia has made significant progress in education since its independence, there are still some schools that lack teaching facilities. In addition to that, it has been estimated that only 49.6 % of teachers are well-qualified, and, according to the Vision 2030 report, only 2% of school-leavers will acquire a university education. By 2030, Namibia wants to provide unified and adequate education to all regions, train well-qualified teaching staff, and improve early childhood education as well as research and development centers.

Namibia also plans to develop a highly-productive workforce which will be able to compete both in domestic and foreign markets. The government wants to create a democratic political system with effective institutions in order to guarantee peace and political stability. Additionally, by 2030, Namibia plans to provide affordable health care services to all people. Nevertheless, the problems posed by HIV/AIDS to public health in Namibia should not be overlooked. The government sees combating this disease as a major challenge as to foster the proper development of the Namibian society.

Business under the Economy

Namibia is one of few nations in sub-Saharan Africa that does have to cope with the fallout of chronic economic instability. It qualifies as a middle-income country with per capita GNP figures of US$5,400. This is largely because Namibia is one of the largest exporters of non-fuel minerals in Africa, one of the largest producers of diamonds in the world and one of the world's top uranium producers while the oil industry is a major foreign exchange earner. Five major multinational oil giants control the production, distribution and marketing of petroleum and petroleum products.

Apart from its mining and oil industries, Namibia has a thriving chemicals industry. The manufacturing industry is small and focuses primarily on food processing and beverages. Despite all this, the vast majority of its people continue to eke a living from subsistence agriculture, animal husbandry and forest produce. The rich-poor divide is extreme as the money is concentrated in the hands of a few - mostly white industrialists.

Business Guide

The Government of Namibia is encouraging and promoting foreign investment in an effort to develop the economy, generate employment and boost foreign exchange earnings. Keeping this in mind, the government has taken a number of positive steps to establish a system and environment conducive to foreign investment.

Standard western business etiquette works just fine in Namibia " prior appointments should be made, punctuality is appreciated and business cards should be exchanged. Business apparel should ideally consist of suits in winter and safari suits in summer. English is widely spoken in business circles and is also the official language in Namibia. The best time for business is between February to May and September to November. Offices work from 8 am to 5pm, Monday to Friday.

Lightning Source UK Ltd.
Milton Keynes UK
UKHW020744191021
392466UK00013B/899